CW00594653

A Christia...

Family Planning

Paulette,

Trusting that with this book
and the help of the Lord we
will arrive at a decision that
will be best for us.

Del

1 COR 7 V1-5

Christian Woman books

CREATIVITY
Using your talents
Eileen Mitson and others

FAMILY PLANNING
The ethics and practicalities of birth control methods
Gail Lawther

A WOMAN'S PRIVILEGE
Jean Brand

Other titles in preparation

Family Planning

The ethics and practicalities of birth control methods

GAIL LAWTHER

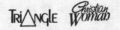

First published 1985
Triangle
SPCK
Holy Trinity Church
Marylebone Road
London NW1 4DU

Copyright © Gail Lawther 1985

All rights reserved. No part of this book may be reproduced or
transmitted in any form or by any means, electronic or
mechanical, including photocopying, recording or by any
information, storage or retrieval system, without permission in
writing from the publisher.

British Library Cataloguing in Publication Data

Lawther, Gail
    Family planning: the ethics and practicalities
    of birth control methods. – (A Christian Woman book)
    1.   Birth control – Religious aspects –
    Christianity
    I. Title   II. Series
    261.8'3666   HQ766.2

    ISBN 0–281–04160–1

Typeset by TJB Photosetting
Printed in Great Britain by
Hazell, Watson & Viney Limited
Member of the BPCC Group
Aylesbury, Bucks

Contents

Editor's Foreword

Christian women are developing a new awareness of the way our faith touches every part of our lives. Women who have always lived in a Christian environment are facing up to the important issues in the world around them. Women who have found in Christ a new direction for living are seeking to sort out the problems that are hampering their spiritual growth. And many women are rediscovering the joy in using their God-given talents, in their relationships with God and with other people, and in their spiritual lives and worship. *Christian Woman* magazine has been privileged to be part of this learning process.

As a result of this deepening awareness and commitment to Christianity, many books have been published which help women to sort out what God can do for them as women, as wives, as career people, as mothers, as single women. Most of these books however have been rooted in the American culture; this *Christian Woman* series has come into being because we believe it is important that we have books that talk our own language, and are relevant to everyday life in our own culture.

Each book in this series will deal with some aspect of living as a Christian woman in today's world. I am delighted that we have been able to be part of the blossoming of God's church in this way. We hope that the books will help you as a Christian woman to overcome problems, enrich your life and your relationships, learn more of God, think through important issues, enjoy your femininity, make wise choices, and deepen your commitment to Jesus Christ.

In these books we have invited people to share what they have learned about living as Christians. Not everyone will agree with all the ideas expressed in each book, but I know that you will find every book in the series interesting and thought-provoking.

Books change people's lives – perhaps these books will change your life.

GAIL LAWTHER

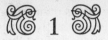

Why read this book?

Why have I written a 'Christian' book on contraception?

The idea began when I was working for a secular book company several years ago; part of my work at that time involved detailed research into new methods of contraception that were being tested around the world. I had always been interested in the practical and ethical problems posed by established methods of birth control, and as I researched further I realized that the new methods were adding both new benefits and new problems to the general debate. At the same time in talking with other Christians I discovered that there was considerable ignorance as to how some birth control methods actually worked.

I felt that it was important to bring the two elements together, especially as contraception is an accepted part of most Christian marriages. I wanted to put in a Christian light the detailed information on various birth control methods that many people are looking for, but which is usually available only in secular books. My husband and I took part in the trials of one of the promising new contraceptives, which increased my interest still more. I originally planned to cover the subject in a series of articles, but soon realized that it would be impossible to do justice to the broad range of birth control methods available – so a book was born. What am I trying to do with the book? Here are some of its aims.

To enlighten Christians

As I mentioned, most of the detailed teaching on how birth control methods actually work is only available in paramedical literature, completely divorced from any spiritual context. Most Christian books on marriage and sex contain a section on contraception, but this is necessarily brief. Contraception is a common part of the thinking of the Western world, and this book aims to provide helpful information for the many, many Christians who are using or planning to use contraception. The actual mode of working, the *accurate* effectiveness (not wishful thinking), and the risks and benefits of traditional and new methods are set out clearly so that they can be compared and assessed.

To avoid some common generalizations

Certain methods of birth control gain particular reputations which are then difficult to shake off. Some of the commonly-held views include: the pill is easy and no-risk; the pill is always dangerous; sheaths are 'dirty'; rhythm methods are useless; rhythm methods are one hundred per cent reliable; IUDs are trouble-free; vasectomy makes you impotent. I hope that this book will show that such generalizations are unhelpful and rarely true.

To help couples choose

I hope that this book and the information it contains will help couples to talk about their attitudes to contraception and to make an informed choice about which method(s) would suit them at their particular stage of marriage. I hope that couples will be able to discuss the subject freely and in depth, as it will affect two of the most important parts of their marriage: their sex life, and the number and timing of any children they have. Couples need not be confined only to traditional methods of contraception; the information on new methods will help to show that there are many feasible options for regulating fertility.

This book is aimed at Christians who are married, or who plan to marry, and are thinking of contraception within the marriage relationship. I am an unashamed advocate of marriage: I am also an unashamed advocate of marriage as the only worthwhile context for a sexual relationship. Therefore I do not deal with casual sex, or sex outside marriage.

2

As a result, any accidental pregnancies referred to are those which have occurred within marriage and a normal sexual relationship – this book does not cover conception which is a result of rape, adultery or sex before marriage.

I have chosen the title carefully, as not all methods of birth control are actually contraception. *Contra*ception means preventing unplanned conception of a child, and is morally very different from ending a pregnancy which has already begun. There is a great deal of confusion over this; the word contraception is used as a blanket term to cover all methods of birth control, and many people have unwittingly used methods which actually prevent a successful pregnancy rather than preventing conception. That is one of the main reasons this book was written: to point out exactly how each method of birth control works.

In order to show all the methods in balance against one another, and to enable couples to make a fully informed choice, I have included details of methods which personally I consider morally unjustifiable. This is because Christianity is a religion of personal responsibility. My responsibility in writing this book is to present the facts as they are presently understood and bring them to people's attention; your responsibility as a user of contraception is to weigh up these facts and make your own decision in the light of them.

I'm sure that I will receive considerable criticism as a result of this book. This will mainly be from people who have already thought through some of the issues of birth control, and who have come to conclusions which differ from my own. For instance, some people will feel that I am overreacting against IUDs and similar methods. Others will feel that I shouldn't advocate contraception at all. Still others will be angry because I point out that there are problems with the pill, and problems with the rhythm methods. However, I feel that many ordinary Christians will be very grateful for the book. They will be those who are using, or want to use, a method of contraception, but who don't really know what all the options are, how reliable they are,

3

and how they have their effects. I hope that many Christian couples who are concerned to make the right choices with each other and before God, will find this book helpful and informative.

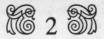

Why choose contraception?

Why might a Christian couple consider using contraception within their marriage? After all, the human race got by for thousands of years before effective means of birth control were introduced, so why the sudden apparent indispensibility of controlling your fertility?

Of course there is no doubt that a lot of the recent interest in contraception in the Western world is linked with sex outside marriage; people are constantly hunting for ways of making this 'safe' from unplanned pregnancy. However the history of contraception is grounded in wanting each married woman to be free to enjoy her marriage, love her husband and plan their children without the constant fear of pregnancy and the drain on finances and health caused by frequent childbearing. You have only to read through the correspondence received by many of the early pioneers of contraception, for instance Margaret Sanger and Marie Stopes, to see the human misery produced by these conditions. Similar conditions are met in many developing countries which have not yet become contraceptively aware. Widespread contraceptive awareness is one of the factors which has helped us in the West to plan our children, improve our living conditions, and provide adequate food, money and education for our children. But there are other reasons for choosing contraception, too.

Sex is good
I feel very privileged that I have been part of a generation of Christians who have been taught that sex within marriage is a good and beautiful gift from God. As a result my

husband and I have been able to enjoy the sexual side of our marriage with great pleasure and freedom. I can only guess at the frustration and guilt that must haunt many people from other generations in the church who inherited the 'sex is bad' teaching. This erroneous teaching persisted for many generations, first of all in the idea that sex itself was sinful, and then in the milder (but still damaging) idea that sex was dirty. This is still a difficult concept for Christians to shake off entirely; we see so much perversion of sex in the world around us that it is hard to enjoy it unrestrictedly ourselves at times.

Try this little test. If you are married: are you able to praise God together for his gift of sex after you have made love? If you are planning to marry: can you pray together and thank God for the sexual union he is going to give you? Even in these more open days many Christians will still flush and clear their throats over such ideas, and say, 'Well ... I, er, can't *quite* do *that* yet ...'. And yet sex within marriage is one of God's most wonderful gifts to us. An illustration in Gavin Reid's *Starting Out Together* puts this perfectly; it is a letter to God which begins: 'Dear God, thank you for our lovely wedding present ...'

There are several books available which give detailed teachings on how the Bible sees sex within marriage as good – I will not cover all the same ground, but here is a lightning tour of what the Bible says. First of all, sex existed before the Fall, and was part of God's very good creation (Gen. 2.23-5). Any teaching which attempts to show sex as only linked with sin, or something which only happened after the Fall, is unbiblical. Sex within marriage was one of the first blessings that God gave to the human life he had created. Sex is not bad or dirty in itself (although it can be made both bad and dirty), and so there is no need to feel any guilt over sexual desire and expression within marriage. It is contrary to the Bible's teaching to feel that abstaining from sex, or only taking part in it as an unpleasant duty, is more holy than enjoying it fully.

Secondly – and this is very important to the issue of contraception – sex is good in itself, not just as a means of producing children. The whole of the Song of Solomon is full of frank but beautiful references to the pleasures of the sexual relationship. The American Lutheran Family Life Committee put it this way: 'The sheer delight of sex is the obviously dominant theme of the Song of Solomon.' Proverbs 5.15-19 is another celebration of a lifelong sexual pleasure in your marriage partner, and 1 Corinthians 7.2-5 shows that the sex relationship is one of constant mutual giving and gratification.

Certainly, children may well arrive as a result of sexual union, but the gift of sex is a gift in itself. It is just as valid for childless couples, couples past childbearing age, handicapped couples and couples waiting before having a child as it is for couples who are trying to conceive. As Herbert Miles says in *Sexual Happiness in Marriage*: 'It is unthinkable for husband and wife to refrain from sexual intercourse except for procreation.' A good sexual relationship is one of the basic keys to a truly happy and stable marriage, as it expresses so much more than just the temporary physical unity. 'It is not just togetherness, but it fosters togetherness' (Herbert Miles). The sexual union is something to be enjoyed and explored with delight, including when the couple is not planning to conceive a child just then, and contraception helps make this unrestrained enjoyment a possibility.

Freedom

The use of contraception also helps to release couples from the pressures of too many children, or ones that arrive too soon. Many young couples are hard-pressed financially, especially in the early years of marriage; the arrival of an unplanned baby, even though it will probably be much-loved, can cause great hardship. This is also true of 'extra' children who arrive after the parents already have as many children as they can cope with. A reliable form of contraception is a great help in these situations.

The early years of marriage are crucial to the wellbeing of that couple's future, and most couples find it best, if at all possible, to avoid having children while they establish the basis of their marriage and sort out problems. Many Christian counsellors recommend that couples use a very reliable method of contraception for the first year at least, so that they are free to form a relationship with one another. Remember that once you have begun to have children, you are not going to have the special freedom of just being a twosome for many long years to come. It is important that a marriage is built on strong foundations, and a very early baby can rock those foundations to the core.

In contrast, some couples choose to have a child or several children very early on in their marriage. Unless they want to bear very many children, this then presents the other side of the problem: what do they do when they have reached the desired number, but the woman still has many fertile years before the menopause – possibly as long as twenty years? An added problem with this situation is that the risks to the health of mother and baby during pregnancy and childbirth grow as the woman gets older. Such couples again will tend to be looking for a very reliable form of contraception.

Health
The health of the mother and any children is an important consideration when thinking about contraception. One of the benefits of contraception is that it allows couples to space children so that there is time for the mother to recover physically and emotionally between pregnancies. It also means that, if the mother is breastfeeding, one child can enjoy all the benefits of breast milk and suckling without having to be weaned early to make room for the next baby. Subsequent children will also be healthier if the woman is not worn down by constant childbearing.

Mental health, or psychological wellbeing, is another factor relevant to contraception. As we have seen, an unplanned baby or constant childbearing can put enormous psychological pressure on the mother – and on the father too, as he struggles to feed, clothe and protect his family. In addition, the fear of unplanned pregnancy can be very real to many women, and should not be taken lightly. Some women are reluctant to accept their status as adult, responsible sexual beings, and the thought of becoming a mother terrifies them. Others are very scared of the idea of pregnancy and childbirth. Such women need time so that they can relax in their roles of wife and lover and be gently prepared for the prospect of childbearing. Other women dread the demands that a second or subsequent child would make if it came along too soon, especially if the first child is very demanding. Still others, who have had a bad experience of pregnancy or childbirth, are terrified of a possible repeat performance if they get pregnant again. Such women can be greatly reassured, and helped to enjoy their marriage and their sexuality, by a reliable means of contraception.

Population control

So far, I haven't mentioned contraception as a means of helping control world (or national) population. Christians have very mixed views as to whether this in itself is sufficient reason for limiting a family. Some feel that it is our responsibility as world citizens to take a part in limiting the world's population explosion. In the Western world we use far more than our just share of world resources; if we have children, they will find it very difficult not to continue this trend. If we live in the developing countries, we may bear children without having the resources available to keep them alive and well. In previous centuries, couples needed to have many children in order to ensure that some survived, and would contribute to the family income. In these days of better nutrition and medical care, it is rare for children to die before adulthood, and so such a high birth rate is not necessary in the same way.

9

From the opposite viewpoint, other Christians point out that God has commanded us to 'be fruitful and increase in number; fill the earth and subdue it' (Gen. 1.28). They feel that God has not annulled this command, and that Christians should continue to have several children. Tim and Beverly La Haye advocate having four or five children, as an interpretation of Psalm 127.35 – the 'quiver' mentioned was traditionally considered to hold five arrows. Others are not so literal, and simply advocate abundance in childbearing – either that we shouldn't limit it at all, or that we shouldn't limit it much. Naturally it is important for any Christian couple to weigh up these pros and cons and seek to find out what God is saying to them particularly.

Childless by choice?

A thorny problem which exercises many Christians is: is it acceptable not to have any children at all, by choice? Many couples (as many as 1 in 6) are unable to have children, or to have all the children that they want, but is it right as Christians to choose a childless marriage?

Once again opinions differ. Most Christians agree that marriage and sex are not just for producing children – but are they valid choices on their own, without ever intending to have children? Gavin Reid mentions in *Starting Out Together* that he feels except for reasons of health or age, couples should not choose childlessness. Tim and Beverly La Haye feel the same: 'We feel that every Christian family should plan on having children if at all possible.' They point out that conditions today are morally no worse than those of the early Christian era, and that it is 'the cry of unbelief' to say that we cannot face bringing up children in today's world.

Other writers do entertain the possibility of choosing childlessness. Anne Townsend (*Marriage Without Pretending*) and John Noble (*Hide and Sex*) point out that if this decision is taken it should be with the full agreement of both partners and in total peace before God. Christians

10

often cite selfishness as a reason for not having children. Certainly it is more than possible to choose childlessness for selfish reasons. What is easy to forget, however, is that it is also very common to choose to have children for selfish reasons. These may be as mild and natural as wanting an outlet for our extra love, wanting someone who will trust us totally, and wanting the experience of pregnancy. The reasons can also be not so admirable: wanting a child to try and heal a fractured marriage; to use as emotional blackmail; to get attention that we feel we've been missing out on; or to have someone that we can control or who will live out our unfulfilled ambitions. These motives are not confined to non-Christians. John White in *Parents in Pain* exposes many of the unworthy reasons why Christians and non-Christians alike choose to have children. Some couples choose childlessness because they don't wish to pass on, or risk passing on, a serious medical condition such as brittle bone disease, haemophilia, Friedrich's ataxia etc. The same can be true of some severe inherited mental illnesses. This is never an easy decision to come to, especially when the couple desire children very much.

So don't condemn out of hand Christian couples who have made a mature decision before God that they feel they can serve him better without children. Christians are quick to tell infertile couples how much more opportunity they have to serve the Lord without the ties of children; exactly the same holds true of those who are childless by choice.

Is contraception biblical?
Does the Bible say anything about contraception? There is only one detailed reference in the Bible to avoiding pregnancy, and that is the story of Onan (Genesis 38). This story has often been used to condemn contraception, as Onan was put to death by the Lord for allowing his semen to fall on the ground rather than allowing it to father a child. But as many Christian writers have pointed out before me, the Bible is quite clear that Onan's sin in the eyes of the

11

Lord was that he refused to carry out his legal duty under the laws of the time, to give a child to his brother's wife.

The Bible does not specifically advocate contraception, but it certainly doesn't condemn it either. We need to weigh up the special importance that the Bible gives to sex within marriage, as an expression of the couple's love, commitment and joy in one another and not just a means of procreation, and the responsibility God has given us to govern our own actions thoughtfully, prayerfully and responsibly. Then, as Herbert Miles says, a couple may marry with confidence that 'the intelligent use of contraceptives ... is definitely within the framework of the plan of God and basic Christian principles.'

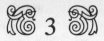

3

How do we choose a contraceptive?

There are three main categories of people who choose to use contraception. First there are starters – those who have not yet had a child, and who want to delay a while before they start having children. Secondly there are spacers, those who have had one or more children, and who plan to have another one or more, but who want to wait a while in between. Thirdly there are the stoppers, those who have had all the children they feel are right and who don't plan ever to conceive again. Couples who choose childlessness are a mixture of the first and last categories – they haven't yet conceived, but they don't plan to in the future.

These varying reasons for contraception have very different effects on such things as how efficient a method the couple wants, how motivated they will be to use it correctly (or at all), how they will cope with an unplanned pregnancy. Age is also an important factor, and so is the length of time you have been married. For instance, a couple who marry at eighteen and don't want their first child yet are different from a couple who marry at thirty and don't want to conceive immediately. A couple who have been married for five years will be more relaxed with each other sexually and less embarrassed about using methods such as caps and sheaths than two young newly-weds. Also a couple of thirty who have not yet had children present different requirements from a couple of thirty who have four children.

The failure rates of different methods of contraception are an important factor – again, more important to some couples than others, and more important at some stages of an individual marriage than others. An unplanned baby whose arrival would be near-disaster after ten months of marriage may be accommodated without a second thought after ten years; or a baby that would have been welcomed at twenty-five may cause great strains if it arrives at thirty-five. It is vital to remember, when you are considering the effectiveness of various contraceptives, that the failures are not statistics. They are pregnancies – unplanned babies which have to be faced up to and coped with. The success rate of many contraceptives depends a great deal on motivation; the more complicated the method, the more this holds true. Caps require more motivation than pills; rhythm methods require more motivation than caps. If it is very important to you not to get pregnant at a particular time, for example in early marriage, in late marriage, while one of you is finishing education, or during financial hardship, then either use a very reliable method or use a less reliable method very conscientiously. Poor contraceptive protection (and lots of pregnancies) can come from using an inefficient method, or using an efficient method carelessly.

There are various kinds of risks which have to be balanced against one another when making your choice of contraceptive. Some methods involve a risk, great or slight, to the health of the husband or wife. Others involve a high risk of pregnancy, which in itself may expose the mother to physical problems or cause emotional or psychological strain on the marriage. A third type of risk is to the health of any child conceived accidentally while using the method. The moral and ethical considerations of the various methods are also very important, and the practicalities of different contraceptives need to be considered carefully.

The possible physical risks of the method of contraception are not the only matters to be taken into account, although they are usually the ones which get the most publicity. Several researchers have pointed out that the 'safest' contraceptive plan, that with the smallest risk of danger to the woman and the highest protection against the birth of unplanned babies, is for the couple to use a simple barrier

14

method and then for the woman to have a legal abortion if she becomes pregnant. Obviously this idea is horrific to most couples, not just to Christians, but it is the safest – therefore safety is not necessarily the factor of paramount importance, or this would be the preferred choice. All of the relevant factors have to be weighed and pondered and discussed prayerfully, so that you choose a method you are both happy with before God.

It can seem that there is an overt concentration on the woman as the one responsible for contraception. This has happened for various reasons. It is the woman who becomes pregnant, and so she has a greater natural reason for choosing to delay pregnancy if the couple is not ready, or if she wants to recover her health between babies. She is also released by effective contraception from the constant fear of pregnancy, and free to enjoy lovemaking. Women have been striving for several decades to gain their true, biblical freedom to enjoy their sexuality.

In addition there are purely practical reasons for concentrating on the woman's system when thinking about contraception. It is far easier to suppress or protect from fertilization twelve or thirteen eggs every year than it is to suppress or restrain the millions of sperm that a man manufactures every day. Nevertheless, contraception is *always* a concern for both partners; it takes two people to conceive a baby, and the co-operation of two people to prevent conception. Contraception will be most effective when both partners are equally happy with and committed to the chosen method, and any extra effort or consideration that it involves. A woman who is always expected to assume the responsibility for choosing and using contraception without the support of her husband will soon become resentful of his seeming lack of care and concern. The marriage as a whole will be on a much better foundation if this aspect, as any other important part of the marriage, is shared.

So how should you choose the method that is right for you at this stage of your marriage? There are several things that you will find helpful. Read carefully through all the sections in this book and see what impression you receive of each method as a practical, moral and effective form of contraception. You may already have a method or two in mind, but do read about the alternatives too; some methods might be easier or more complicated than you imagined, or have practical or ethical implications you hadn't realized. Talk to sympathetic Christian couples; it's not an easy subject to bring up, but many couples who are already married are open to sharing their experiences with particular methods of contraception, and their advice can be invaluable. If you know a Christian doctor trained in family planning, talk to him or her as well. If you want to use one of the methods that requires medical or other trained supervision, then talk to the appropriate family planning practitioner. You may discover that you are medically unsuited to a particular type of contraceptive; the details listed under each method will probably give you a clue about this. An absolute contraindication for a method means that under no circumstances should you use it, as it will present a grave risk. A relative contraindication means that it may be feasible to use the method if you are kept under close medical supervision, or if you take extra health precautions, or it may mean that another method is more suitable.

Also, pray together to ask God to show you which way of regulating your fertility he wants you to use at this stage. Your choice now doesn't have to be your choice forever; many couples use a variety of methods at different stages of their marriage. Finally, it is very important that you talk honestly together over some of the implications of contraception, having children, pregnancy etc. Here are some of the questions you can usefully ask yourselves and each other; the honest answers may surprise you as much as they surprise your partner.

Do we want to have children?   YES

16

Honeymoon Baby. if not within 6 months, if not 26 April. if not asap.

If so, when? *↗*

How important is it that we don't conceive before then? *VERY*

What will we do if we conceive an unplanned baby? *KEEP IT*

Does either of us want to complete any education or training before we have a child? *NO*

How many children do we want eventually? *2.*

How far apart do we want them? *2 minutes/9 months*

Are there any methods of contraception I instinctively dislike? *The Pill*

Are there any methods I instinctively favour? *NO (Sheath!)*

Will the method we're considering make sex less pleasurable for either of us? *Don't know!*

Do we have any absolute contraindications to the method? *NO*

Are we emotionally suited to the method? *I THINK SO*

Are there any dangers to an unborn child? *NoNe*

Are there any undesirable side-effects? *NoNe*

Do I feel at peace with myself about this method? *YES*

Do I feel at peace with God about this method? *YES*

Does my partner feel at peace with this method? *DON'T KNOW!*

Will this method be inconvenient to obtain? *DON'T THINK SO!*

Will this method be expensive? *NO*

What are the alternatives? *DON'T KNOW*

Once you have pondered these matters and read the different sections, the questionnaire on p.149 may help to point you towards the most suitable contraceptive(s) for you at the moment.

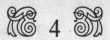

4

Interrupting conception and pregnancy

THE PROCESS OF CONCEPTION

Conception, or fertilization, is the fusing of an ovum (egg) and a sperm to form a new human life. This can only happen at a certain stage of a woman's menstrual cycle, and if certain other conditions are fulfilled also. It is useful to understand the process of conception so that we can then see how the process can be interrupted.

Menstrual cycles vary a great deal from woman to woman, but there are certain factors that all normal menstrual cycles have in common. The first day of a menstrual cycle is the first day of a woman's period (bleeding from the vagina). This bleeding is the uterus shedding its thickened lining. During the next two weeks or so the brain's hypothalamus will stimulate the pituitary gland to produce hormones. One of these, the follicle stimulating hormone (FSH) stimulates the development of several follicles (egg-cases) in the ovary. The other, the luteinising hormone (LH), makes the follicles produce oestrogen. Oestrogen in turn stimulates the uterus to start building up its lining to prepare to nourish a baby.

In the middle of the woman's cycle (around day 14 in a 'textbook' 28-day cycle), the level of LH reaches a very high peak, which stimulates the dominant follicle to release an egg; this is known as ovulation. The ruptured follicle is now called a corpus luteum ('yellow body') and begins producing progesterone as well as oestrogen. Around the time of ovulation the basal (resting) body temperature drops slightly and then rises significantly immediately afterwards, and maintains a higher level for some time. The cervix (en-

18

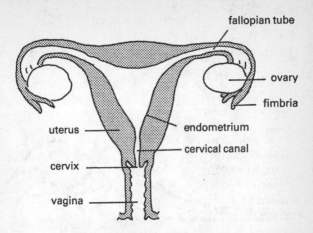

Female reproductive tract

trance to the uterus) becomes soft, the cervical canal opens wider, and the cervical mucus becomes clear and slippery so that sperm can penetrate it.

If pregnancy does not occur, the corpus luteum degenerates after about ten days; when this happens oestrogen and progesterone levels fall rapidly. The hormone levels are then not high enough to maintain the thickened endometrium (lining of the uterus), and this is sloughed off as menstruation. Then the whole process begins again. If pregnancy does occur, the corpus luteum is preserved by the presence of a further hormone called human chorionic gonadotrophin (HCG); this is produced by the placenta. Between six and eight weeks into pregnancy the placenta is capable of producing sufficient oestrogen and progesterone to maintain the pregnancy, and the corpus luteum slowly degenerates as it is no longer needed.

Fertilization usually occurs in a fallopian tube. When the egg is released by the ovary the fimbria (finger-like projections at the ends of the tubes) sweep the egg into the entr-

Changes experienced through a normal monthly cycle

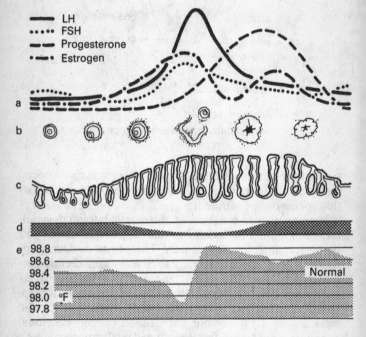

(a) Hormone levels
(b) Follicle and corpus luteum
(c) Endometrium
(d) Cervical mucus
(e) Basal body temperature

ance of the tube. Minute hairs (cilia) push the egg slowly down the tube towards the uterus. The full journey takes about three days, but the egg is only ripe for fertilization for about twenty-four hours, so the sperm have to travel all the way from the vagina up to the outer end of the fallopian tube. This is a hazardous journey, and sperm need to be tough and healthy to survive it. A man's normal ejaculate contains several hundred million sperm, but only a few hundred will make it anywhere near the egg.

Sperm are produced in the man's body by the action of hormones on the testes. Once the sperm are made they are stored for a while; the whole process from the beginning of manufacture until ejaculation is about three months. Just before orgasm the sperm are diluted with various lubricants and the resulting liquid, the semen, is ejaculated from the tip of the penis during intercourse. This means that the semen forms a pool around the cervix at the top of the vagina.

During most phases of the menstrual cycle the cervical mucus is hostile and impenetrable to sperm, but around the time of ovulation it becomes thin and slippery; this makes it into an ideal environment for the sperm to swim through. In addition the cervical canal widens, which helps the sperm to penetrate into the uterus. Chemical conditions in the cervical canal help to kill off weak or damaged sperm, and also help prepare the healthy sperm for fertilization. This is the process known as capacitation, and is vital for conception; sperm which have not been capacitated cannot fertilize an egg.

The tails of the sperm lash them forward in a swimming motion into the uterus; from the uterus they will then enter the fallopian tubes. (Of course, roughly half the sperm will be going on a wild goose chase up the wrong fallopian tube!) By this stage many of the sperm will have died off, and many others will do so during the journey up the fallopian tube. Only the very strongest will reach the egg, and of those only the first will be able to fertilize it.

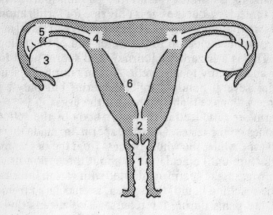

Stages in conception:

1 Sperm are deposited near the cervix.
2 Sperm swim through the cervical canal
   and undergo capacitation.
3 An egg is released from the ovary.
4 Sperm swim up the fallopian tubes.
5 Sperm and ovum meet high up in one
   fallopian tube and fuse.
6 The fertilized ovum travels down the
   fallopian tube and implants in the
   endometrium.

The first sperm penetrates the outside of the egg, and the genetic material from sperm and egg fuses to produce a new, unique human life. The sex of the child is determined by whether the sperm was carrying an x (female) or a y (male) chromosome. As soon as fertilization takes place with one sperm, chemical changes rapidly take place which prevent any other sperm from joining in.

The fertilized egg cell (sometimes called a blastocyst or zygote) soon begins to divide; this happens about once every twenty-four hours, so that it is two, then four, then eight cells and so on. While this is happening it is continuing its journey down the fallopian tube to the uterus. Meanwhile the uterus is receiving signals that fertilization has taken place, and completes its preparations as a hospitable environment. When the fertilized egg arrives in the uterus it implants itself in the enriched endometrium (uterus lining); this is the process known as implantation, or nidation. If all is well, the fertilized egg continues to develop into a full-grown baby, nourished via the placenta for around nine months until it is ready to be born.

INTERRUPTING THE PROCESS

There are five possible stages at which the process of conception and pregnancy can be interrupted:

1 There is no egg available to be fertilized.
2 No sperm are introduced into the woman's reproductive system.
3 The sperm and the egg are prevented from meeting.
4 Implantation of the fertilized egg cannot take place.
5 The pregnancy is aborted.

The various methods of birth control are planned to work at the following stages:

Stage 1: combined pill; mini-pill (in part); breastfeeding; rhythm methods; long-acting hormonal methods (in part).

Stage 2: vasectomy; sheath; withdrawal; male pill; vaccination against sperm.

Stage 3: Caps; mini-pill (in part); long-acting hormonal methods (in part); sponges; douching; spermicide; female sterilization; intra-cervical devices; vaginal ring (in part.)

Stage 4: IUDs; mini-pill (in part); long-acting hormonal methods (in part); vaccination against pregnancy; post-coital IUD; post-coital pill; vaginal ring (in part).

Stage 5: abortion; menstrual extraction.

RELIABILITY OF THE MAJOR CONTRACEPTIVES

There are often large discrepancies between different people's estimations of how effective a particular method is. This can be due to bias – for instance if one person feels that the pill is the easiest and safest method for most women, he or she may well overplay the failure rates of the barrier methods. Also, trials may have been done with women or men who are already fully committed to the method and trained in it, which does not give a fair picture of the average success of the method as used by average ordinary couples. However, there are two generally accepted methods of presenting failure rates, based on clinical trials.

The first is the *theoretical failure rate*; this is the estimated rate assuming that everyone uses the method consistently and accurately and follows all the related instructions. The second figure is the *actual failure rate*; this is based on typical users and assumes an element of human error; for instance some people will forget to take a pill, or will decide to take a risk and not use a cap or sheath. Both figures are given as failure rates per hundred woman years (HWYS) – the number of pregnancies that can be expected in a hundred women using the method for the first year.

Obviously some clinics feel that certain figures are more accurate than others; this list is based on the figures of

Hatcher *et al* (see bibliography), which is one of the most highly respected annual digests of contraceptive technology.

Method	Theoretical failure rate (or lowest observed rate) per HWYS	Actual failure rate per HWYS
Female sterilization	0.04	0.04
Vasectomy	0.15	0.15
Injectables	0.25	0.25
Combined pill	0.5	2
Mini-pill	1	2.5
IUD	1.5	4
Sheath	2	10
Diaphragm plus spermicide	2	10
Cervical cap	2	13
Spermicide alone	3–5	15
Rhythm methods	2–20	20-30
No method of contraception	90	90

CONTRACEPTIVE USAGE IN THE UK

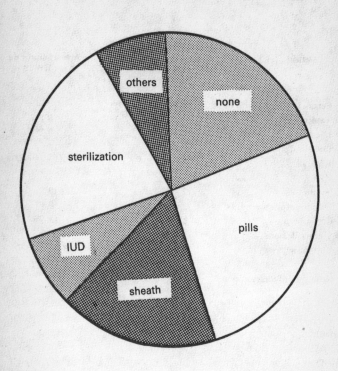

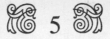

5

Unreliable methods

Several of the oldest known methods of contraception are still practised by millions of couples worldwide; these are withdrawal (coitus interruptus), breastfeeding, and douching. Although there is no doubt that among them they have significantly reduced the number of babies produced worldwide, they are unreliable methods for individual couples who are definitely trying not to conceive.

WITHDRAWAL

This is also called coitus interruptus or 'being careful'. It involves the man withdrawing his penis from the woman's vagina before he ejaculates, so that as few sperm as possible ever enter the vagina. Withdrawal is thought to be still the third most popular form of reversible contraception in this country (after the pill and the sheath). Advantages of the withdrawal method are that it is readily available at any time; requires no medical intervention, hormones or mechanical devices; and costs nothing.

Disadvantages are that it is an unsatisfactory conclusion to lovemaking, and that it has a high failure rate. The sex act is designed by God to be completed with the husband's penis inside the wife's vagina; the time of togetherness after orgasm, while the physical union is still complete, is one of the most precious parts of lovemaking. Occasionally it may be desirable to forego this full satisfaction, for instance if the woman is ill and cannot take part in full intercourse, but constantly to cut the sex act short every time you make love is frustrating to man and wife and not to be recommended. It can prevent the woman from achieving orgasm, and can be very difficult psychologically for the man, whose urge before ejaculation is to penetrate deeper rather than to withdraw. It is particularly difficult for any man who suffers from ejaculatory problems, or who has poor ejaculatory control.

When used consistently, withdrawal has a theoretical failure rate of 16 per 100 woman/years. The actual failure rate is 23 per 100 woman/years. Most failures result from inconsistent or incomplete use of the method in the heat of the moment. Consequently it is not a good method if it is important that you don't conceive.

You may nevertheless find withdrawal a useful method for a limited time, for instance when you have gone on holiday without your cap, or when you are trying to space babies. If you do use this method occasionally, make sure that any fluid is wiped from the tip of the penis before it enters the vagina. Although it is unlikely that pregnancy will result from such a small amount of semen, it is still possible, especially if the man has recently had an orgasm as those few drops will then be full of sperm. If you withdraw too late, then an immediate application of spermicidal foam will somewhat diminish the chances of conception, but many sperm are already likely to be inside the cervix and the foam will not reach them. The main conclusion is that withdrawal is an unsatisfactory method of birth control, which is more successful at increasing the gap between pregnancies than avoiding them altogether.

BREASTFEEDING

Once again, worldwide, this method of contraception can take the credit for keeping the birth rate lower than it might be otherwise. However, like withdrawal, it is far more effective at increasing the time between babies than at preventing them altogether. Many, many couples have been let down by relying on breastfeeding as an absolute contraceptive.

Lactation delays, but does not prevent, the return of ovulation after childbirth by reducing the body's luteinising hormone which stimulates ovulation. Women are infertile for the first four weeks after childbirth, particularly if they are breastfeeding. If *full* breastfeeding continues, i.e. if milk alone is given to the baby, on demand, round the clock, this time may well be extended. Most people will know a couple who did not conceive for many months while the woman was breastfeeding; most people will also know a couple who conceived by accident when the woman was breastfeeding. Many cases in which the mother weans a baby early (with the loss to that baby of the continued benefits of the breast milk and breast contact) are because the woman has discovered that there is another child on the way.

At the moment it is impossible to predict just when after childbirth a particular woman will ovulate. Nearly eighty per cent of women ovulate *before* they have their first period after childbirth, so it is no good waiting for this sign before you start using contraception. The contraceptive benefit during breastfeeding occurs because the decrease in LH inhibits ovulation, but it may not prevent it completely. Reduction from full to partial breastfeeding often causes the menstrual cycle to resume, if it hasn't already.

If you are breastfeeding, don't rely on this as an absolute method of contraception. If you are happy to take a chance, then you can increase the contraceptive effect by breastfeeding fully, on demand, round the clock. If it is important that you don't become pregnant again straight away, then use an alternative method of contraception. Barrier methods, mini-pills, spermicides and sterilization are all good alternatives, although a cap may be difficult to fit immediately after childbirth.* IUDs can also be used during the later weeks of breastfeeding, although I wouldn't recommend them. The combined pill should not be used, as

---

*Some clinics are reluctant to perform sterilization this soon after birth in case the baby falls victim to cot death or any other early tragedy, in which case the parents may wish to have another child.

it reduces the quantity of milk produced.

DOUCHING

Douching consists of washing out the vagina with water or another liquid. Despite popular belief to the contrary, it is not a method of contraception. It is possible that if a thousand women douched after sex and a thousand didn't, then perhaps not quite so many of the douchers would get pregnant. However, once you have had sex millions of sperm swim *immediately* into the cervical canal. All the douching can do is wash out any that are left in the vagina; the others are likely to be heading towards your fallopian tubes with grim determination. By all means douche after sex if you like – this is a common feature of some cultures – but don't expect it to have any contraceptive effect!

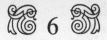 6

Barrier methods

Barrier methods of contraception are so-called because they prevent the sperm from meeting an ovum by placing a physical barrier in between. Barrier methods are some of the oldest forms of contraception; scientific and medical research has now removed much of the guesswork of old barrier methods, and made their modern equivalents very efficient at preventing conception.

The barrier between the sperm and the ovum is often a thin membrane of latex or rubber, worn by the man as a sheath over the penis, or by the woman as a cap over the cervix. A new barrier method – a variation of the oldest – consists of a small sponge placed high in the vagina. The barrier may also be formed by a layer of foam, cream or jelly, which also contains spermicidal chemicals to incapacitate or kill the sperm. The most effective barrier contraception combines two of these methods, for instance the sheath plus foam or a cap plus spermicidal cream.

To anyone who accepts the theory of contraception, there are no real ethical problems posed by barrier methods. They do not alter the body's hormones, or necessitate sexual abstinence, or cause early abortions instead of preventing conception. None of the barrier methods has been given anything like the amount of medical research allocated to the pill and IUD, because they are generally classified as 'non-medical' methods. Therefore it is difficult to say with absolute certainty that barrier methods have no medical side-effects. However, caps and sheaths have been in use for so long, and have been used by so many millions of people throughout the world, that it is unlikely that this is so – any links would surely have become evident as a consistent pattern in barrier method users.

One study reported in 1981 did cause concern as it seemed to link the use of spermicide near conception with an increase in congenital malformations of the foetus. Theoretically, a sperm which has travelled through a layer of spermicide could have been damaged, thus altering its pattern of chromosomes. However, the *Which? Guide to Birth Control* described it as a study which 'unfortunately … raised more questions than it answered'. For instance, the rate of malformation in spermicide users was 2.2%, while it was 1.1% in the control group – but the national rate of congenital malformation is 2.1%. Also, those studied were couples who had had a prescription for spermicide in the previous two years; there was no definite proof that the spermicide had been used at or near the time of conception. The general consensus among contraceptive experts is that the matter should continue to be studied, but that there is at the moment no cause to believe that spermicide can damage the developing foetus.

The problems relating to barrier methods are not so much ethical as practical, mechanical and aesthetic. Some couples dislike the thought of using any mechanical device to prevent conception. If a sheath, or spermicide alone, is used, then contraceptive precautions have to be taken actually at the time of lovemaking. Some women are unhappy about touching their genitals, and so may find inserting a cap distasteful. All the barrier methods require some kind of preparation for sex; some can be rather messy! A couple thinking of using a barrier method consistently should look very carefully at the requirements and mechanics of the chosen method, and decide whether they are acceptable, and whether they are willing to establish or alter their patterns of lovemaking accordingly.

All barrier methods are useful for couples who don't want to use the pill or IUD, or for those for whom the pill is unsuitable, e.g. older women, those with a history of heart or circulatory disease. As with many methods of contraception, the success of barrier methods depends very much on the motivation of both partners involved. It is easy to be irresponsible, forgetful or erratic over using barrier methods, which can result in a high failure rate; on the other hand, when used conscientiously barrier methods can have a very low failure rate. Also, there is no problem with re-establishing fertility when a couple wants to conceive a baby after using a barrier method; both husband and wife remain fertile throughout the time of using the contraception.

THE SHEATH

The sheath is a tube with one closed end, which is worn over the penis during sex to trap the sperm and prevent them from entering the woman's vagina. Sheaths are also commonly called condoms, rubbers, skins, French letters and Durex (after one of the main brand names).

The first sheath was described by Fallopius in 1565 – he developed a linen bag for protection against syphilis. The famous lover Casanova popularized sheaths, but they did not become readily available until the discovery of vulcanized rubber in the mid nineteenth century. Up till then, sheaths had mostly been made of animal intestine or skin. The wider use of sheaths and coitus interruptus (see p. 27) in Britain at the end of the nineteenth century probably accounted in part for the drop in the birth rate at that time.

Modern sheaths are generally made of rubber (although a small number are manufactured from animal collagen), and modern technology means that the rubber can now be very thin indeed. There is very strict quality control for sheaths manufactured in this country; they are checked rigorously for flaws or for weakness, and must conform to British Standard 3704 (look for the kite mark on the packet!).

Sheaths can be obtained in various shapes – ribbed, plain, teat-ended etc. They are all a standard size, approximately seven inches long, as they can expand so much (up to six times their original size). Some sheaths are pre-lubricated; these are claimed to increase the man's sensitivity. Some brands are advertised as being spermicidal; these contain a small amount of spermicide in the lubricant. The *Which? Guide to Birth Control* says 'this may provide some extra protection, but is unlikely to be quite as effective as a traditional spermicide used together with an ordinary condom'.

Sheaths are generally packed in foil, which keeps them in good condition; if stored away from heat, humidity and friction they have a 'shelf-life' of several years. However, excessive heat or humidity can cause the rubber or package to deteriorate. Similarly, carrying a sheath around in a pocket or wallet for very long can damage the packaging with a similar result. Sheaths should never be lubricated with petroleum jelly, as this damages the rubber; if you require extra lubrication, use KY jelly.

The sheath is one contraceptive which has to be fitted at the time of sex, as it has to be fitted on an erect penis. Before *any* penis/vagina contact, remove the sheath from the packet. Unroll the first inch; if the sheath does not already have a teat end to catch the sperm, pinch the end with the thumb and forefinger. This will leave an empty pocket to hold the sperm, and will also help prevent any possibility of bursting. Unroll the sheath fully onto the erect penis – this can be done by the man or the woman; if it is not fully unrolled, semen may seep out of the bottom of the sheath. Make sure that you do not damage the rubber with your fingernails as you unroll it. The sheath must be put on before any contact with the vagina, as even the drops of lubricating fluid produced by the penis before ejaculation contain many sperm. After ejaculation, and before your erection subsides, hold the sheath close to the penis with your fingers and withdraw both carefully from the vagina, making sure that no semen escapes.

Advantages

Over 2 million men in Britain use the sheath regularly. There are many advantages; for instance, sheaths are easily available over-the-counter, and do not need any fitting or prescription by a doctor. Indeed many large chemists' now have sheaths on display at the counter so that customers can serve themselves and just present the goods for payment rather than having to ask for them. Obtained in this way they are fairly cheap; they can be bought even more cheaply by mail-order in bulk. Family planning clinics can provide sheaths free of charge, but they cannot be obtained on prescription from your GP.

As far as can be determined, sheaths produce no serious physical side-effects for either partner, or for any baby conceived accidentally if the method fails. In addition, they help prevent the spread of some forms of VD. There is also evidence that use of the sheath (or cap) helps protect the woman from cervical cancer; recent research suggests that this condition is triggered off by frequent exposure of the cervix to semen (especially that of multiple partners). The sheath prevents the semen from ever reaching the vagina.

In these days of more openness about sex, sexuality and contraception, the sheath provides a form of contraception which both partners can take part in using – many couples incorporate putting on the sheath into their foreplay before intercourse. And, of course, one of the main benefits is that used conscientiously, especially with a spermicide, the sheath has a good success rate as a contraceptive.

Disadvantages

Some of the main disadvantages of the sheath are that the couple always needs to be prepared for intercourse, and that putting on the sheath must always be done at the time of sex, which may reduce the spontaneity of lovemaking. Consequently this is not a good method to use if you or your partner are embarrassed over sex or contraception, as it is very difficult to put on a sheath and apply spermicide unobtrusively. Sheaths can be slightly embarrassing to purchase and carry around, although probably no worse than spermicide or the pill. The sheath is the only reliable non-medical contraceptive that gives responsibility to the man and there is no doubt that many men don't want to take this responsibility.

Most men find that even the best sheath dulls their sensitivity somewhat. The degree varies. For some men it makes sex with a sheath unacceptable; for others it is no particular problem, and for those who suffer from premature ejaculation it can be a positive advantage. Some women may also find their sensitivity during lovemaking decreased. Another disadvantage is the need to withdraw the penis and sheath as soon as intercourse is over – this can bring the intimacy of lovemaking to a rather abrupt end. Disposal of the sheath can be a problem, as they tend to block the drains if flushed away; throwing them away with the rubbish is preferable.

A few men and women develop allergies to compounds in the rubber or the lubricant of sheaths. This can often be remedied by switching to another brand, or by using the more expensive collagen sheaths. Another problem that many people find difficult to overcome is that sheaths still have a slightly furtive, squalid aura about their use. This feeling is quite unnecessary in the modern day, when sheaths are a respected and reliable contraceptive. In other countries the sheath has no such associations; it is estimated that in Japan, four out of every five men use sheaths as their regular contraceptive.

Reliability
Sheaths should ideally be used with a spermicide as this makes them far more reliable. If used this way, the woman should insert a suitable spermicide (preferably foam) about ten minutes before intercourse. If used with foam, the theoretical failure rate can be as low as 1 per user/year (2-3 without spermicide). The actual failure rate is more like 5 per user/year with spermicide and approximately 10 with-

out. The three largest surveys of sheath use had failure rates of 11, 14 and 14.9; smaller studies have varied from 3 to 36(!).

One reason for failures of this contraceptive method is poor quality sheaths; not all the sheaths on sale in this country are manufactured here, and so may not conform to our stringent standards. However, the most common reason for failure is intermittent use, or when the couple decides to take a risk rather than interrupt the spontaneity of love-making. Once again, statistics vary a great deal according to the care and commitment of the users.

Conclusions
Used conscientiously in conjunction with a spermicide, the sheath is a reliable contraceptive with a good success rate. It is also very good for intermittent use, for instance to cover the 'unsafe' days in the rhythm methods, after childbirth, while the woman is changing contraceptive methods, as a back-up when a woman has forgotten to take a pill, or when a man is waiting for the 'all-clear' after a vasectomy. It is best used by couples who are fully at ease with their own and each other's bodies, who have little or no embarrassment about obtaining and using it, who do not find it aesthetically unacceptable, and who experience no physical problems (e.g. allergy, lack of sensitivity) with the method.

CAPS
Caps are female barrier methods designed to prevent sperm from entering the cervix (see p. 19). There are several different kinds of cap, but all work on the same basic principle: a dome of thin rubber or plastic holds spermicide against the cervix, so that any sperm reaching that region are killed or blocked. It is important to remember that caps are not intended to work by physically blocking off the cervix – the contours of the vagina make this very difficult to do effectively. They work mainly by holding spermicide against the cervix, where it is most needed – this is why they should always be used with spermicide for maximum effectiveness.

Early prototypes of caps were known in many parts of the world. China and Japan used discs of oiled silk paper; women in Europe and the Far East used moulded wax wafers, hollowed-out half-fruits such as lemons, and even small cups. The use of leaves, sponges (see p. 50), wool soaked in oil, and other similar techniques has also been recorded.

The modern diaphragm was invented in 1838, following the discovery of vulcanized rubber, but only became well-known in the 1880s. The name 'Dutch cap' which is sometimes given to the diaphragm comes from the ardent promotion of its use by a Dutch doctor. The diaphragm was very popular with early family planners, because for the first time it gave women control over their own fertility; they did not have to rely on the man abstaining from sex or using contraception himself.

Many women in the 1940s and 50s used caps successfully for the whole of their fertile years. In the 60s and 70s, the era of the pill and the IUD, caps lost popularity because of their relative inconvenience and inefficiency compared with the new methods; caps suddenly seemed old-fashioned. Now, with the swing against the pill and IUD, they are experiencing a relative comeback, although they are still used by only about six per cent of British women who use contraception.

There are four main types of cap. By far the best known and the most widely-used is the diaphragm; most of this section will be concerned with using this type of cap. Other types are the cervical cap, the vault cap and the vimule – these will be covered at the end of the section, as much of their usage is similar to that of the diaphragm.

THE DIAPHRAGM

The diaphragm or Dutch cap (also often called just 'the cap') fits between the pubic bone and the back of the vagina. It is held in place by the vagina's muscles and also by the spring around its rim. There are three types of diaphragm, named according to the type of spring used around the rim. The first kind is the arcing spring; then there is the coil spring, which is particularly suitable for women who have not had any children. The third kind is the flat spring; it can be used by women with poor muscle tone. The diaphragm is a dome of thin, soft rubber. It can be obtained in sizes 50-100mm, which is the measurement of the external diameter of the dome. Although the fitting is fairly

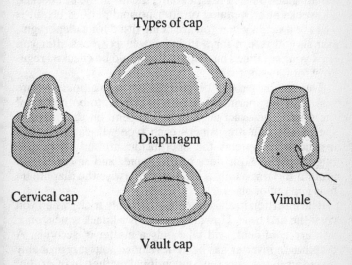

Types of cap

Diaphragm

Cervical cap

Vimule

Vault cap

straightforward, it needs to be done by a doctor or other trained family planning practitioner, to ensure a correct fit. As the vagina expands during the arousal that accompanies lovemaking, the largest comfortable size is chosen. If the diaphragm is too small it may become dislodged during lovemaking; if it is too big, it will be uncomfortable to use.

Most doctors will fit a diaphragm; caps and spermicides can be obtained on prescription or free from family planning clinics. The woman is taught the correct method of inserting and removing a diaphragm of the appropriate size at the first visit, and then is usually asked to return a week later with the cap already in place, so that the instructor can ensure that the diaphragm is correctly positioned. A diaphragm should be checked for fit every six months , as alterations can occur in the body or in the diaphragm itself. The fit should also be checked after any pregnancy (whether it ends in miscarriage, abortion or birth), and after a weight change of more than 7-10lbs (3-4½kg). If the diaphragm is fitted while you are breastfeeding, the fit should be checked six weeks after weaning or after normal periods begin. If you are a virgin when you are being fitted for a diaphragm, you should return for a fitting check six weeks after you start your sex life. The diaphragm should be checked regularly for flaws or tears.

The diaphragm can be inserted up to two hours before sex. Squeeze spermicide cream or jelly onto both sides of the dome; the exact amount will depend on the brand of spermicide you are using – each type will carry its own instructions. Spread the spermicide around with your finger to coat both sides of the dome, and smear a little around the rim – only a little, as otherwise the diaphragm may slip out of place.

The insertion itself can seem impossibly tricky when you try it the first time. However, it is only a knack which, once you are confident, will take only a matter of seconds. A diaphragm inserter has been developed, but it is probably no easier to use than the conventional method of insertion; also it may cause injury to the tender membranes of the vagina if it is not used very carefully. Squeeze the diaphragm at both sides so that it becomes long and narrow (if you have put too much spermicide on the rim, you may find that it shoots out of your hand at this stage!). Insertion is easiest if you stand with one foot on the bed, chair or toilet seat, although once you are confident, insertion can easily be done squatting or lying down.

With one hand, spread the labia apart; with the other, push the diaphragm gently along the vagina and over the

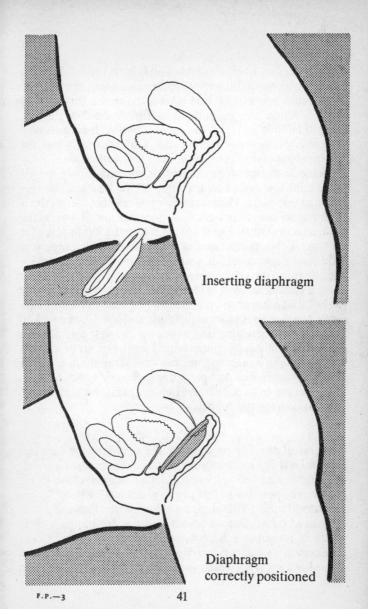

Inserting diaphragm

Diaphragm
correctly positioned

cervix, then release. The rim of the diaphragm springs back into its normal position, and the diaphragm should be lodged in place over the cervix and behind the pubic bone. Check with your fingertip; if the diaphragm is correctly positioned you will be able to feel the cervix through the dome. When the diaphragm is fitted, neither partner should be able to feel it during sex, although occasionally the man's penis may hit the rim. Different positions for lovemaking may make this more or less noticeable.

Some instructors recommend that you insert more spermicide into the vagina as a matter of course once the diaphragm is in place. Others say that you only need to do this if more than two hours elapse before sex, or if you make love a second time. The diaphragm must be left in place for at least six hours after sex; never remove the diaphragm to add more spermicide if you make love a second time – simply place the spermicide in the vagina.

The easiest method of removing the diaphragm is simply to hook one fingertip over the rim and ease the diaphragm out. Again, this is most easily done with one foot on a bed or chair, or when squatting. After use, wash the diaphragm in water; you can use unperfumed soap, but water alone is often enough as the spermicides are water-soluble. Rinse the diaphragm well and pat it dry thoroughly, then store in its container in a cool place. High temperatures and humidity can damage the rubber.

CERVICAL CAP

A cervical cap fits snugly over the cervix like a thimble; although it fits more closely than the diaphragm, it is still generally used with a spermicide. Cervical caps have never been very popular in this country, although Marie Stopes preferred them to diaphragms in her clinics; they are generally used by women who want to use a cap but have difficulty in retaining a diaphragm. Because the close fit over the cervix is vital, cervical caps can only be used by women who have a cervix which is regular in shape, healthy, and

42

easily accessible. The cap is generally made of rubber, with a raised hollow rim. Sizes are measured by the internal diameter of the rim, and range from 22-31mm; the size chosen matches the base of the vaginal part of the cervix.

The cap is smeared on both surfaces with spermicide, and then compressed between thumb and forefinger. It is guided into the vagina and onto the cervix, which can be felt through it. Alternatively, spermicide can be placed inside the dome only, and then a vaginal spermicide added after insertion. Generally the same rules apply as for the diaphragm; the cap can be inserted up to two hours before sex, and should be left in position for six hours subsequently. Some practitioners have claimed that a cervical cap can be left in place throughout the month and only removed for menstruation, but most experts are unhappy with this idea and recommend that it should be removed after each use (although for further developments along these lines, see p.140). The cap is removed by inserting a fingertip under the rim and easing it off the cervix; one type has a hole in the rim for an optional removal thread.

VAULT CAP

The vault cap is bowl-shaped with a thin centre and a thicker outside. It has no rim, but is held in place by suction. Sizes vary from 50-75mm (the outside diameter of the rim); the correct size is the smallest one that fits evenly. The vault cap is not as easy to use as the diaphragm, but can be useful for women whose vaginal muscles are weak or whose cervix is damaged. Spermicide is put on the inside and outside of the cap, but not on the rim as this would spoil the suction. The cap is inserted, and when it is in the correct position the centre is depressed with a fingertip; this expels air and produces the suction to hold it in place. Like the other caps, the vault cap should be inserted not more than two hours before sex and left in position for six hours subsequently. One difference is that the downward straining of a bowel movement while you are wearing the vault cap may break the suction and dislodge the cap, so it is always worth checking that it is still in place afterwards.

VIMULE CAP

The vimule cap is shaped like a deep-brimmed hat, and is a cross between the cervical and vault caps. Once again the cap is held in place by suction, and can be useful for women who cannot hold other types of cap in place, for instance those with poor or damaged vaginal walls. Instructions for using spermicide, insertion and removal are similar to the other small caps; as with the cervical cap, a thread can be attached to help removal.

Advantages
Like other barrier methods, caps are good choices for couples who don't want to use an IUD or hormonal methods, and who don't want to practise periodic abstinence from sex. One enormous advantage of caps over sheaths and spermicide alone is that caps don't have to be inserted at the time of intercourse, so there is no interruption of love-making. (Of course they *can* be inserted during lovemaking if you prefer, or if you are not already prepared.) The caps themselves and stocks of spermicide are available on pre-scription or free from family planning clinics. The choice of different types of cap means that many women could use a cap successfully if they wanted to.

There is some evidence that using a cap reduces the trans-mission of some kinds of VD and also that, like the sheath, a cap reduces the risk of cervical cancer by keeping the semen away from the cervix. As with other barrier methods, there is no problem re-establishing fertility when a pregnancy is desired, and no known risk of harm to either partner. There is also no reason to suspect that using a cap can cause any damage to a baby conceived after (or while) using this method of contraception. The need to use sper-micide is often helpful to women with little natural lubri-

44

cation, although some men and women find that the amount necessary actually decreases their sensations. Caps can be very useful if you are making love during a period, as they hold back much of the menstrual flow. In addition, caps, when used conscientiously, are a fairly successful means of contraception.

Disadvantages
Like other barrier methods, using a cap requires that you must prepare for sex each time, and carry the cap and spermicide with you when you go away. Any people who find a 'mechanical' method of contraception unpleasant are likely to dislike the preparation, insertion, removal and washing routine of caps. It can be difficult to keep the method private, because of supplies of spermicide around the house, washing the cap after sex etc.; some parents may find this embarrassing.

A cap needs to be fitted by a trained person, and cannot be bought over the counter. Some women cannot wear a diaphragm, particularly those with an unusually-positioned uterus, a prolapse (where the uterus has slipped down the vagina because of poor muscle tone), a rectocele or cystocele (a bulge in the vaginal wall from the urethra or intestine). It is also true that using a diaphragm can aggravate problems of the urinary tract, such as cystitis; all women are encouraged to empty their bladder regularly while wearing a diaphragm. Happily, many of these problems can be overcome by using one of the other types of cap. Some sexually inexperienced women may find the psychological or physical relaxation needed for insertion difficult to achieve; some few women may be allergic to one component of the rubber used in the cap.

Reliability
The diaphragm is the cap most commonly assessed regarding success and failure rates, as it is the most commonly used. Reliable studies have shown failure rates as low as 2

per 100 woman/years, which is the theoretical failure rate of the diaphragm with spermicide. The actual failure rate has been as high as 29 in one study, with an average of 10-15. This is really a very large difference. Most pregnancies arise because the woman was not instructed properly on how to fit the diaphragm correctly, or because the diaphragm became damaged, dislodged or mis-shapen, because the cap was removed too early, or, more commonly, because it was only used intermittently and couples decided to take a risk.

Failure rates are highest among new users, especially those changing from a more 'automatic' method such as the pill or IUD. The longer a women has been using a cap, the fewer the unwanted pregnancies – this is probably a combination of factors. The older woman is probably more experienced in the technique of insertion, she is more mature and takes fewer risks, and her fertility is lower than that of a younger woman. Regarding the other caps available, the cervical and vault caps show similar success rates to the diaphragm when they are used with spermicide. So far, there do not seem to be adequate data for the vimule. As with many other methods, the successful use of a cap depends very much on the motivation and conscientiousness of the user, and the skill of the instructor.

Conclusions

Caps, when used conscientiously, are fairly successful methods of contraception. The best candidates as cap users are women who don't want to use the pill or IUD or rhythm methods, who are at ease with their own bodies and don't mind the mechanics of insertion and removal, and who are happy, with their husbands, to include regular use of the cap in their sex life. Women who have cultural, social or personal taboos about handling their own body, or who dislike having to take active responsibility for contraception, are likely to find using a cap distasteful and will probably not be enthusiastic users even if they have a cap fitted.

Caps are good contraceptives for women approaching the menopause, as fertility is reduced then while the risks of the pill are increased. If it is important that you don't get pregnant, then you will need to use the cap with great dedication – and even then you might not be successful. Like the sheath, the cap is an excellent back-up method for pill emergencies, between other methods, before operations (when you have to come off the pill), and when waiting for a clear sperm count after a vasectomy. It is also a very useful method for nursing mothers, and is a good tide-over for the 'unsafe' days of rhythm methods.

SPERMICIDES

Over the years, numerous substances have been tried to prevent fertilization, including ox blood, cow dung, vinegar, lemon juice, oil and honey. Serious widespread research started only in the 1930s, and in the subsequent years there were many brands available. With the advents of the pill and IUD interest waned, and there are now comparatively few brands on the market.

Spermicides combine two agents: a chemically inert blocking material, which physically impedes the sperms' progress, and a second substance which chemically destroys or immobilizes the sperm. Most brands are based on nonoxynol-9, which coats and breaks down the surface of sperm cells. Spermicides come in various forms: cream, jelly, pessary, aerosol foam, foaming tablets and water-soluble film. The exact method of use depends on the type used. Foaming tablets and melting pessaries or suppositories require three to twenty minutes to disperse, depending on the brand used. The water-soluble film can be placed in the vagina or over the tip of the penis. Jellies and creams really rely on the thrusting of the man's penis for full distribution. Foam is used from an aerosol can; the can needs to be shaken fully to ensure that the spermicide is well mixed and aerated. With most types a separate applicator is filled from the nozzle of the can, although some brands come pre-filled. The applicator is inserted far back into the vagina and the plunger pressed. This can be done immediately before intercourse, or up to thirty minutes previously. If you use foam it is best always to keep a spare container in the house, as there is often no warning that one is about to run out. All spermicides deteriorate in time, or if the container becomes damaged or the material becomes too hot or cold; so take careful note of any 'use by' date, and store in a dry, reasonably cool place.

Advantages
Spermicides alone are one of the few methods of contraception available without any medical intervention. Spermicides are available over the counter at chemists', and require no prescription – although they can also be obtained on prescription, and free from family planning clinics. Spermicides alone have remained a reasonably popular contraceptive alternative as they are less bulky to carry around and less complicated to use than when combined with a cap or sheath.

Spermicides act as good lubricants for sex, which can be an advantage if the woman's membranes are fairly dry, for example during and after the menopause. There is no difficulty in re-establishing fertility when a pregnancy is wanted, and no evidence as yet of any medical risks to husband or wife. Some spermicides also offer some protection against some forms of VD – evidence suggests that they can restrict the growth of organisms causing gonorrhoea and genital herpes.

Disadvantages
Spermicides alone need to be used at or near the time of intercourse, which can interrupt the spontaneity of lovemaking. They also inevitably increase the vaginal discharge after sex, as they add to the seminal fluid and the woman's secretions – with a sheath or cap, either the semen or some of the spermicide is contained inside. Warm and

humid climates can cause handling problems with creams and melting pessaries, as they begin to liquefy; this can be remedied by running them under cold water before use.

Although the modern spermicides are all tested chemically, some can still produce irritation in either partner. If this does happen, changing to one with a different chemical base may help. Recent research has shown that nonoxynol-9 is absorbed through the vaginal mucous membranes, which has led to some concern that this could damage the woman, or a child if she is breastfeeding. This area is being researched further. Finally, there can still be some embarrassment over buying spermicides, although many large chemists' display them for self-selection to ease this problem.

Effectiveness

The theoretical failure rate for spermicides alone can be as low as 3 per 100 woman/years, but actual failure rate is much higher. Studies over the last fifteen years have produced failure rates of up to 29, with an average of about 20 (although the *Which? Guide to Birth Control* is more optimistic, and says about 10). Failures occur both when the spermicide is used, and when couples decide to take a risk and not use it. Foams are the most effective spermicides, probably because they are immediately distributed across the cervix. Foaming tablets and melting pessaries can fail to disperse properly. Jellies and creams are not intended for use on their own (they are designed for use with a cap or sheath), but because they too are on sale without prescription they are often used alone and are not as effective as other spermicides. Also, because creams and jellies are mainly distributed by penile thrusting, pregnancy can occur if the husband suffers from premature ejaculation, before the spermicide is well distributed. Soluble film is very difficult to position correctly, whether it is used by the man or the woman, and is not as effective as foam.

Conclusions

Don't use spermicide alone if it is important that you don't conceive! The failure rate is too high to take risks with. On the other hand, if it would not be too disastrous if you conceived, and you don't like the pill and IUD and don't want to bother with a cap, sheath or rhythm method, then spermicide alone will certainly give quite a few women a fair degree of protection against pregnancy. This method is not a wise choice for a newly-married couple, who would have to worry about the messy mechanics of using spermicide as well as about the high failure rate, but it could be a perfectly good method for a couple who have had one child and are not too bothered when the next arrives. It is also a very good back-up method for emergencies when a sheath splits; applying foam immediately can help to prevent pregnancy.

Couples are more likely to use this method conscientiously when it is for a limited time, so it can also be a good method for unprotected days before a packet of pills takes effect, or if one pill in a cycle is forgotten. However, the general consensus is that spermicides are far more effective when combined with a cap, sponge or sheath. One of the main functions of the cap and sponge is to hold the spermicide over the cervix, where it is most needed, which is difficult to achieve with spermicide alone.

SPONGES

Sponges are a modern reworking of an ancient method of contraception – women used to dip a small piece of natural sponge into oil or some other agent, and insert it into the vagina. The Today sponge, which is now available over the counter, is quite a breakthrough in barrier methods. It is a soft domed disc of polyurethane sponge about 5cm in diameter, shaped to fit snugly over the cervix; it has a tape across the back for removal. The sponge is impregnated with 1g of spermicide (good old nonoxynol-9 again). Before use the sponge is taken out of its plastic sachet, dipped in water, and inserted into the vagina; the woman positions it over the cervix with her fingertips.

The sponge has to be left in place for six hours, like a cap, but can then be removed and thrown away – it is disposable. However, it can be left in place for up to two days with no extra spermicide. Some practitioners have suggested that it can even be washed and re-used once or twice, although eventually the spermicide will be washed out, but this is not recommended by the sponge's developers. The sponge cannot be used by a woman who has a prolapse of the uterus or very poor muscle tone in the vagina, as the sponge would not stay in the correct position. Because the sponge doesn't need to be covered with spermicide it is much less messy to use than a cap. It needs no prescription, and unlike caps does not have to be fitted by a trained practitioner; the Today sponges are all the same size. American trials suggested that the sponge was as reliable as the diaphragm, but the major British trial suggests that it has roughly twice the diaphragm's failure rate, possibly as high as 25 pregnancies per 100 woman/years. Unfortunately, the current high retail price of the sponge could cancel out the benefit of its ready availability.

The sponge

Hormonal Methods

Hormonal methods of birth control work by changing the body's hormone levels either so that conception is prevented or so that the body is made unsuitable for sustaining a pregnancy. The combined pills (commonly called just 'the pill') are the best-known hormonal contraceptives. Other oral contraceptives (those taken by the mouth) are the mini-pills, or progestogen-only pills. Hormonal methods also include hormone implants, hormone-releasing IUDS, and long-lasting injections, all of which are now quite well-established methods of birth control, and also newer areas of research such as the male pill, vaginal rings, hormonal nasal sprays etc. (see p. 145).

There is considerable controversy in Christian circles over the ethics of various hormonal methods of birth control. First and foremost is the Roman Catholic Church's objection to any 'artificial' methods of birth control (i.e. anything other than the rhythm methods). Interestingly, one of the main developers of the contraceptive pill and its use was Dr John Rock, himself a Catholic. The official teaching of the Catholic Church inevitably proscribes the pill, although some Catholic individuals find no objection.

Some Christians of other denominations disapprove of the pill because it interferes with the body's natural processes. This is undoubtedly true; the combined pill supplants the body's own rhythm with a similar, but infertile, rhythm that is artificially produced. Since the pill is taken by healthy women who are functioning normally, some people feel that it is wrong to interfere with the body in this way. I have great sympathy with this view on an individual level – I fully understand any woman deciding that she doesn't want to alter her body in this way. However, I feel that there is no reason for a blanket condemnation of the pill just because it does this. We all alter our body's natural rhythms by all kinds of everyday activities such as drinking tea and coffee, watching an exciting film, taking exercise. The fact that the pill alters natural body rhythms is not sufficient reason to condemn it.

A charge often levelled at hormonal methods of contraception is that they are not 'natural'. This is generally quibbling over words. No form of contraception is strictly natural: if things were left to nature, women would get pregnant far more often than they do. John Guillebaud, who is this country's leading authority on the pill (and who also is a committed Christian) points out that in some ways the pill is more 'natural' than non-hormonal methods. The usual course of events in a past or present society that is not contraceptively aware is that married fertile women have a baby roughly every year. Between the birth of one and conception of another they are usually breastfeeding, and so often do not have sustained cycles of ovulation and menstruation for years at a time during their fertile life. Guillebaud points out that the pill actually imitates this 'natural' cycle far more accurately than barrier methods, IUDs or rhythm methods, as it too suppresses the cycle of ovulation and menstruation. Contraception to some extent is bound to be an unnatural process, and if all other factors are equal no one method can strictly be described as more or less natural than any other.

Another feeling about the pill is that it introduces lots of artificial chemicals into the body. This is less true than many people realize – the elements of combined pills, oestrogen and progestogen, are very similar to the oestrogen and progesterone produced by the woman's body. In fact, if they were not virtually identical in structure the body's chemo-receptors would not accept them into the system. The reasons that synthetic hormones are used are that they are cheaper, and also they are not broken down by the body when taken orally. Early trials had to use injections rather than pills until it was discovered which compounds could be taken successfully by mouth. However, these early trials showed that the contraceptive effect was just as good with the naturally-occurring hormones as with the synthetic substitutes that were developed later. The difference could perhaps be compared with using artificial colours instead of crushed precious stones to make paint; the final result is just as good, but the synthetic version is cheaper and easier to produce.

The pill has rather suffered from being blamed for the permissive society. It is quite true that ready availability of the pill made promiscuity more tempting as it offered widespread protection from pregnancy. However, just because something can be abused it doesn't necessarily mean that it is wrong in itself – that is rather like looking at the spread of gambling and saying 'there, I knew money was wrong'. Money can be used for good or for ill; so can contraception, the pill included.

Having looked at some of the ethical questions raised by the idea of hormonal contraception, what about the ethics of the way each method works in controlling the birth rate? Here I feel there is an important distinction between the combined pill, or its derivatives, and the other available hormonal methods – mini-pills, implants and injectables.

The ordinary combined pill, which contains oestrogen and progestogen, acts mainly by preventing ovulation. This means that no egg is released at any stage of the cycle, so of course there is no chance of one being fertilized. Combined pills which are low-dosage (50mg or less of oestrogen) are thought to be only 95-98% effective at inhibiting ovulation. In these cases the rest of the contraceptive effect is supplied by lesser changes resulting from the hormones: the cervical mucus becomes both physically and chemically virtually impassable to sperm, and inhibits sperm capacitation (see p. 21). Therefore using a combined pill, in the very unlikely event of an egg being released, it is extremely unlikely that it would be fertilized. For people who accept hormonal contraception, there are no ethical quarrels against the use of the combined pill.

The case is very much more complicated, however, in hormonal contraceptives which use progestogen only. It is mainly the oestrogen which suppresses ovulation; mini-pills, Depo-Provera (the most common injectable) and NORPLANT (the most common implant) use only progestogen. To some extent progestogen is responsible for preventing fertilization, by making the cervical mucus inhospitable and by inhibiting capacitation to some extent. However, its back-up effect in most progestogen-only contraceptives is to inhibit implantation of the fertilized ovum in the uterus, by changing the nature of the endometrium (uterus lining). This means that if you believe that life begins at conception, progestogen-only methods can cause early abortions in the same way as IUDs. The sperm and the ovum have joined and a new life has started, but it cannot implant successfully in the uterus and so is discharged from the body. The evidence that this method works *solely* by preventing implantation is much less clear-cut than that for IUDs, which seem from recent studies generally to work in this way; in fact it is unlikely that progestogen-only methods do rely mainly on this factor. However, it still plays a large part in the methods' successes. This needs to be considered carefully and prayerfully by any couple thinking of using the mini-pill, Depo-Provera or implants.

The other area of ethical concern over hormonal methods is the attached health risks. Only some health risks are associated with progestogen-only methods, which is why some couples choose these methods in preference to the pill as they do not understand the way in which the progestogen acts. Far more attention is paid to the health risks of combined pills as (a) they are better documented, (b) the risks are greater, (c) many more women use them, and (d) they affect far more of the body's systems than progestogen-only methods.

A contraceptive which makes periods lighter and virtually pain-free, which is extremely reliable, which is dissociated from sex itself and which helps protect the user against several forms of cancer, anaemia, duodenal ulcers, pre-menstrual tension, toxic shock syndrome, vaginitis, ectopic pregnancy, endometriosis, benign breast disease and arthritis would be very good news. The pill is such a contraceptive. However, a method which increases the risks of weight-gain, high blood pressure, heart attacks, strokes, thrombosis, gallstones, malignant melanoma, liver tumours and cystitis would be pretty bad news. This also is a description of the pill.

Many of the undesirable side-effects of the pill would be tolerated virtually unquestioningly if the medication were being taken to save life – for instance if it were a treatment for heart failure or leukaemia. In particular the possible mild side-effects such as weight gain or headache would probably be tolerated quite happily. However, because the pill is (or should be) taken by healthy women, they need to decide whether it is the benefits or the risks which weigh heaviest in their thinking. Obviously there is no substitute for careful medical assessment of the woman's health and medical history, and the preferences and priorities before God of the couple concerned, for deciding whether or not a particular woman is a good candidate for the combined pill. I don't want in any way to underestimate the possible risks for some women taking the pill. On the other hand, here are some factors which help us to see the debate in its most accurate light, and may help you in deciding whether or not you want to take the pill.

1 Many of the studies on the pill have been done on women who have exclusively or for part of the time been taking pills containing far higher levels of hormones than are now prescribed.

2 It is the studies themselves which have helped to

identify women who are at risk from the pill; these days most such women are never given the pill at all.

3   The pill is an extremely reliable contraceptive.

4   The risks of the pill must be carefully weighed against the risks of becoming pregnant, which is a very real possibility if you use a less reliable contraceptive instead. Presently, the chance of dying as a result of pregnancy or childbirth is 1 in 10,000 in the UK (1 in 500 in a developing country). The chance of dying as a result of taking the pill is 1 in 77,000 for non-smokers under the age of thirty-five, who are the women most likely to be given the pill.

5   The pill is less dangerous than many other risks taken commonly by many of us. For instance, you stand a greater likelihood of dying if you regularly go swimming or drive a car than if you take the pill.

6   Your doctor will tell you if you have any known conditions which are likely to make pill-taking dangerous for you.

COMBINED PILLS

Combined pills, containing oestrogen and progestogen, are commonly referred to simply as 'the pill'. Worldwide there are currently 50-60 million women using the pill, and it is still the commonest method of contraception in the United Kingdom (the sheath is a close second). It is particularly popular with young women; up to seventy per cent of sexually active women in their twenties use the pill in this country.

For centuries women (and men) have been searching for an oral contraceptive. In ancient China it was recommended that the woman swallow twenty-four live tadpoles in the early spring; this was said to prevent conception for five years! All over the world primitive peoples have believed that certain plants prevent pregnancy. Some of these plants have been shown to contain oestrogens, so may have some genuine effect; others may work in a totally different way. Many others probably don't work at all. However, the World Health Organization has a task force researching into plant products to see if any of them have usable contraceptive properties.

In the early 1900s it was conclusively shown that action of the corpus luteum (see p. 18) in a pregnant woman prevents further pregnancies from occurring. In 1921 an Austrian doctor suggested that extracts from the ovaries of pregnant animals might prevent pregnancy in humans. It was not until the 1930s that there was sufficient understanding of when in the menstrual cycle a woman was most likely to conceive to allow work on altering that pattern to control fertility. By the late 1930s extracts from pregnant rats were being used for experimentation in humans, but they had to be given by injection because the extracts were destroyed by the digestive system.

In 1943 progesterone was produced from a product of the Mexican wild yam, and large trials began in Puerto Rico in 1956. Since the 1960s, there has been a progressive trend towards lower dosages of oestrogen and progestogen in the pills. Dosages of 100-150mcg of oestrogen and 1-10mg of progestogen were common, but levels nowadays are usually 30-40mcg of oestrogen and 1mg or less of progestogen.

How the pill works
It is rather misleading to talk of 'the pill', as many dozens of different brands have been tried in various parts of the world through the years, but all combined pills are based on similar ingredients and work in similar ways. Each pill contains oestrogen and progestogen (synthetic progesterone), which are very similar to the hormones produced by the woman's body. The oestrogen works on the brain's pituitary gland and 'fools' it into thinking that the woman is pregnant. Consequently the pituitary doesn't release its normal follicle stimulating hormone (FSH) and surge of luteinising hormone (LH), which normally stimulates ovulation (see p. 18), so no egg is released.

In addition the oestrogen and progestogen between them make the cervical mucus virtually impenetrable to sperm, interfere somewhat with sperm capacitation, and also make the lining of the uterus inhospitable. Most types of pill regime include a 6 or 7-day pill-free 'resting' phase to imitate a woman's normal menstrual cycle. During this time the thinner-than-usual lining of the uterus comes away and is discharged like a period. This bleeding is really a withdrawal reaction to stopping the oestrogen contained in the pill, and is not a true period; that is why many women on the pill find that their 'periods' are virtually trouble-free.

Preliminaries

If you feel that you want to use the pill, your doctor or family planning clinician will do his or her best to ensure that you are a low risk for any of the pill's possible dangers, and that you understand fully how to use the pill. You will be asked about your medical history, your age, and your smoking habits, and then will be weighed and have your blood-pressure taken. You will also be asked whether you have ever been pregnant, whether the pregnancy or pregnancies ended in birth, miscarriage or abortion, and whether you have ever had treatment for VD or any kind of vaginal or pelvic infection. These questions can be rather distasteful if you are still a virgin, but they are necessary for the doctor to form a complete picture of your gynaecological health.

The doctor will discuss the pill and the way it works with you, and the clinic may prefer to give you an internal examination. This is not vital, but is helpful to the clinician, especially if you are already sexually experienced, as it can help detect problems such as fibroids, ectopic pregnancy and cervical erosion. In this examination the doctor will probably do a manual check of your uterus and ovaries, and will then visually examine the vagina and cervix with the aid of an instrument known as a speculum. If you are sexually active the doctor may well take a Pap smear of the cervix to check that all is in order. Your breasts will also be examined to see if there is any abnormal growth or lumpiness.

When the doctor has made all these checks, he or she will be able to make a very accurate assessment of whether or not you are a suitable candidate for the pill. If you are not, then the doctor will discuss alternative forms of contraception with you. If you are, the doctor will select the pill brand that is best suited to you; this will generally be the lowest possible dose that can be relied upon to prevent ovulation. The doctor will ensure that you know exactly how to take that particular type of pill, and will probably give you only three months' supply to begin with. This is to ensure that you return for a full check-up so that your progress, health and satisfaction with the method can be monitored.

Taking the pill
There are several different types of basic combined pill; some of these require slightly different routines.

The most common pill-taking regime is '21 days on, 7 days off'. Pills of this kind come arranged in a circuit of 21 pills to a packet. Each one is marked with a day of the week, but as each pill contains exactly the same balance of hormones it doesn't matter which you start with. The days are marked only to make it obvious if you have missed a pill. When you have taken pills 21 days in succession, and finished the packet, then you stop for 7 days. During this time you will get a period-like withdrawal bleeding. You are still protected from conceiving during this 7 days, as the hormone levels in your body are still high enough to continue stopping ovulation. On day 8, you begin a new packet of pills, and so on in a 21 days of pill, 7 pill-free cycle. Some pills modify this cycle slightly, and have 22 days on and 6 off. This is simply so that you stop and start your pills on the same day of the week – and it can act as a memory jogger for the forgetful.

For the *very* forgetful, or those who live such an active life that they can lose track of where they are in the cycle, there are 28 day pills. In these packs, 7 of the pills are 'dummies' – they do not contain hormones. These pill systems work just like the basic '21 day on, 7 days off' system, described above, with withdrawal bleeding during the 7 days of taking the dummy tablets. The advantage is that a pill is taken every day, so the woman doesn't need to keep track of when she should be stopping or starting again. The disadvantage is that she has to be careful to start the pack in the right place, otherwise she could take the dummy pills instead of the real ones. The packs are clearly marked to show which is which. Another type of pill is the 'phased' kind. Biphasic pill packs have two different mixtures of hormones for two parts of the monthly cycle. Triphasic pill packs have three different mixtures. These phased pills are intended to imitate the normal menstrual cycle more exactly; because they do this, the dosages of oestrogen and progestogen can be the bare minimum through the month to keep the woman from conceiving. Because they are closer to the normal sequence of hormone rise and fall, the woman's withdrawal bleeds are more like normal periods, and may still have accompanying pre-menstrual tension and pain (these are usually absent with ordinary pills). Of course with phased pills it is extremely important that you take the pills in the correct order. Because the dosage of hormones is so low, there is a very much reduced margin of error if the pills are taken in the wrong order or if one is forgotten. These pills should not be used to change the timing of your period, which can be done with ordinary combined pills (see p.64).

Some pill-taking women prefer what is known as the 'tricycle' system (*not* the same as the triphasic pill). This involves taking four packs of pills in a row without a break, then having a 7-day break. This means that withdrawal bleeding occurs only once every three months. However, it also means that the woman takes significantly more hormones over any given year, and so some doctors advise against this system.

Starting the pill
There are two main ways of starting the combined pill. The traditional way is to begin with the first pill on day 5 of your

cycle (remember day 1 is the first day of your period). It doesn't matter whether or not your period has stopped by then. If you use this way of starting, you will not be protected against conception for the first 14 days, as the hormones are still reaching the correct level. If you are already married, you should use an alternative contraception, or abstinence, for these 14 days. If you are going on the pill prior to getting married, then make sure that you get over this 14 day phase before your wedding!

A newer way to take the pill is to start on day 1 of your cycle (the first day of your period). This gives complete contraceptive protection straight away, and you do not need an alternative method. This can cause a little more 'breakthrough' bleeding in the middle of your first cycle as the hormones adjust. It also means that your first withdrawal bleed will be 21 days after your last period began, so your first cycle will be extra-short. From then on, of course, you will experience a normal monthly pill cycle.

You may want to start the pill after a pregnancy. You are usually sterile for four weeks after a normal birth, so if you are bottle-feeding you can start the pill towards the end of the fourth week, although some doctors recommend a longer wait (see p. 29 for guidelines on breastfeeding and the pill). The pill can be started immediately after a miscarriage or a suction abortion, but some doctors prefer to wait for a month or so, so will recommend an alternative method for that time.

Timing the pill
You should always aim to be consistent in the time you take your pill. If you always take them roughly twenty-four hours apart, then the body should always contain a high enough level of hormones to prevent ovulation. Some doctors recommend that you take your pill last thing at night, but if your routine is too varied to make that feasible, then taking the pill in the mornings will probably suit you better. Consistent pill-taking is very important; if you decide to use the pill then you should be committed to taking it every day

that it is necessary. *The Health Provider's Guide to Contraception* states that 'the efficacy of the method relies entirely on the woman's consistency in pill-taking'.

Naturally, everyone is human and there is bound to be at least one occasion when you forget to take your pill. The rules here apply only to ordinary combined pills; other types of pill (progestogen-only, phased pills) do not have such a large margin for error. If less than twelve hours has elapsed since your proper time for taking the pill, simply take the missed pill as soon as you remember it and carry on as usual. You will still be protected against conception. However, if more than twelve hours has elapsed, take your pill anyway (and carry on taking subsequent ones in your normal regime), but use a back-up method of contraception for the next 14 days. *This is very important.* It is extremely likely that 'breakthrough' ovulation will occur if your hormone level suddenly drops during your normal pill-taking days, and many of the pregnancies that occur in women on the pill occur in this way.

Stomach upsets can also play havoc with the body's absorption of the pill. If you are sick *after* three hours of taking a pill, don't worry – the pill will already have passed into your system. If you are sick *within* three hours, take another pill from a spare pack. If it happens again within three hours, then try again with another one; as long as you can keep one pill down for three hours you will be all right. If you can't, or don't feel like trying, within twelve hours of your usual pill time, then again you will need a back-up contraceptive for the next 14 days (or longer if you miss pills for more than one day). The same is true if you have diarrhoea; the pill is likely to have been passed through your digestion before it has had time to be absorbed. In this case also you will need extra protection for 14 days (or more, if the diarrhoea lasts for more than one day). Antibiotics can also prevent full absorption of the pill, and therefore an alternative method may need to be used while on a course of antibiotics, up until your next withdrawal bleed.

Desirable side-effects

The pill is associated with quite a number of beneficial effects on the body, ranging from the useful to the life-saving. One of the most obvious benefits of the pill is freedom from the fear of pregnancy, which is a very important plus factor to many women. However there are also other, non-contraceptive benefits to some pill-users.

One of the greatest is the regulation of the menstrual cycle. Irregular periods, spotting (mid-cycle bleeding), mid-pain at ovulation, pre-menstrual tension, painful periods and heavy bleeding are all virtually eradicated in most pill-users. However, women with very irregular cycles are not generally considered good candidates for the combined pill. Because the withdrawal bleeding is generally much lighter than normal periods, women on the pill are far less likely than other women to suffer from iron-deficiency anaemia. Another benefit is that women using ordinary combined pills can time their periods to avoid special occasions such as holidays, conferences and, of course, their own wedding days! Pills can only be used in this way to postpone a period, simply by taking the pills for longer than 21 days before a break; they should never be used to try and bring on a period earlier, as this is quite likely to result in ovulation and possible pregnancy. If in doubt, consult your doctor or family planning practitioner.

Pill-takers have a much reduced rate of upper genital tract infections and pelvic inflammatory disease (PID) than women who don't take the pill. This is thought to be because the pill decreases the amount of blood lost during menstruation, which can be a culture medium for bacteria, and because they make the cervix less easily penetrated by germs. Because pills suppress ovulation, the incidence of ectopic pregnancy is very low indeed.

There is some evidence that use of the pill helps to protect against ovarian and endometrial cancer. There is also decreased incidence of ovarian cysts, rheumatoid arthritis, non-malignant breast diseases, duodenal ulcers, toxic shock syndrome and endometriosis among pill-users. Women who already have endometriosis (an unpleasant but fairly common condition which in severe cases can lead to infertility) find that the pill is very effective in treating the condition. The kind of depression and loss of libido that is associated with pre-menstrual tension is often removed completely by the pill. In addition, it is also thought, though not yet proved, that the pill reduces the incidence of trichomoniasis vaginitis (TV), an unpleasant infection. Fibroids are less likely to arise in pill-users, but women who already have fibroids in the uterus may find that the pill aggravates the fibroids' degeneration.

Good or bad?
Some side-effects of the pill vary greatly with the woman who is taking it. Asthma, epilepsy, hirsutism (excess hair), greasy hair, migraine, breast tenderness and skin conditions such as eczema may all be improved or made worse by the pill. This will depend on the woman's body and on the type of pill used. Many of these conditions, if they are aggravated by one type of pill, can be lessened by switching to another under your doctor's guidance. Breast enlargement is a common effect of combined pills, especially in the first few months. For some women this is a boon – for others it is distressing.

Undesirable side-effects
The pill is also associated, directly and indirectly, with quite a few undesirable side-effects. These can range from the irritating to the life-threatening.

Mild side-effects can include headache, photosensitivity (unusual sensitivity to light), extra vaginal discharge through cervical erosion, less vaginal lubrication, and problems with contact lenses because of changes in the fluid over the cornea. Hay fever can begin in sensitive people when they start taking the pill. Moving on to somewhat more serious effects, the pill can occasionally act as a catalyst for unusual conditions such as chloasma (benign pigmented areas on the face also known as the 'mask of pregnancy'), jaundice, gallstones, and benign intracranial pressure. The pill may in rare cases reduce the body's defence against chicken pox, eczema, allergies, gastric flu, malaria and joint inflammations; it appears in some way to alter the body's immune systems. Pill-users may become more prone to cystitis and other similar infections; the urine is thought to become a better culture medium for bacteria, and also pill-users often make love more frequently than other women, and sex can stimulate an attack of cystitis.

Taking ordinary combined pills can interfere with the quality and quantity of milk produced by a breastfeeding mother, and so should be avoided if you want to breastfeed. Your doctor or family planning practitioner will advise you on alternative methods during this time. It appears that loss of scalp hair can occur after some women stop taking the pill, although this is rare. Underweight women are particularly likely to experience nausea during the first few months of the pill; this can be minimized by taking the pill last thing at night, so that you sleep through the worst symptoms, or perhaps by changing to another brand of pill. Some women who are suffering from mild or moderate depression may find that this is aggravated by the pill, although it doesn't appear to aggravate severe depression.

Some women also experience a loss of libido, although others experience an increase. The pill should never be given to girls who have not yet finished growing, as development of their joints can be permanently affected. Some women on the pill experience a milky discharge from the nipples; this should always be reported to your doctor as it may require treatment. In very rare cases pill-users may develop one kind of chorea, uncontrollable movements of parts of their body: this will disappear as soon as they stop the pill.

What about cancer? This is a common fear linked with the pill. At present the news seems roughly balanced between the good and the bad, with a possible bias towards the good. Breast cancer is so common (1 in 11 women in the USA will develop it) that any change made by the pill, however small, would be statistically significant. It seems from present research that the pill may actually slow down the development of breast cancer, although any woman who presently has or who has had cancer should stop taking all hormones except those prescribed by her specialist. One of the latest studies suggests there is no increased risk of breast cancer if the pill is taken after age twenty-five, and no increased risk before that age if the pill is low in progestogen.

There seems to be no link between the pill and cancer of the liver, although long-term pill-users may develop benign liver tumours. Similarly there seems to be no link between pill use and cancer of the cervix (also a very common cancer), except in that widespread use may encourage sex at a younger age, which does increase vulnerability. Cancer of the endometrium was more likely in women who took sequential pills, but these are now not available for this very reason (they are not the same as phased pills). Combined pills actually seem to help protect against this cancer. The strange condition known as molar pregnancy, or hydatidiform mole, is not caused by the pill, but the pill can interfere with its treatment. Malignant melanoma (a type of skin cancer) does seem to be slightly increased in pill-users living in sunny countries.

Potentially life-threatening risks do occur in some users but it's important to remember that the reason for the medical checks is to screen out women who are likely to be at risk. Hypertension (raised blood pressure) is common to a very mild and perfectly safe degree in most pill-users, but can occasionally be severe. Because the pill interferes with the blood's clotting mechanism in several ways, problems of the cardiovascular (heart and blood) system are among the most dangerous potential side-effects of the pill. These can include blood clots in the legs, abdomen, lungs, heart

(heart attack) or brain (stroke).

Virtually all of these conditions are made *far* more likely if the woman smokes. It is important to point out that taking the pill on its own carries a far smaller health risk than smoking on its own. Combined, the two can be very dangerous, but as Guillebaud points out, 'pill-taking makes your smoking more dangerous', not the other way around. A woman under thirty-five on the pill has a 1 in 10,000 chance of dying if she smokes, 1 in 77,000 if she does not. A woman aged thirty-five to forty-four has a 1 in 2,000 chance of dying if she takes the pill and smokes, 1 in 6,700 if she takes the pill but does not smoke. If a woman who smokes wants to go on the pill, i.e. if she is thinking about two different risks to her health, she would do much better to go on the pill and give up smoking than to carry on smoking and use another form of contraceptive. Many doctors are of the opinion that a woman taking the pill should never smoke at all (actually, many doctors are of the opinion that no-one should ever smoke at all).

Heart attack and stroke incidence are increased in pill-users, and also in smokers, but also in women who are over thirty-five, who are very overweight, or who have diabetes, hypertension, or a personal or family history of cardiovascular disease. The more of these factors you combine, then the more likely you are to be at risk if you take the pill. Clots in the legs are more likely if you are overweight, pregnant, diabetic, confined to bed, or undergoing surgery.

Contraindications
So who should avoid the pill? Generally doctors have two classifications: absolute contraindications (women who under no circumstances should take the pill) and relative contraindications (women who may be able to take the pill under close medical supervision). Several relative contraindications together may add up to an absolute contraindication.

Thrombosis, or history of.

Stroke, or history of.

Coronary artery disease, or history of.

Hepatic adenoma, or history of.

Present impaired liver function.

Malignancy of the breast or reproductive system.

Pregnancy or possible pregnancy.

Very severe migraine.

Severe sickle-cell anaemia.

Angina or other heart disease.

Any high risk factors for thrombosis (e.g. abnormal blood fats, severe diabetes, very heavy smoker, aged over forty-five, very overweight, very high blood pressure).

Pituitary gland disorder.

Recent molar pregnancy.

Recent abnormal, undiagnosed uterine bleeding.

History of any serious condition caused by past pill-taking.

Obviously some of these conditions are transient, such as pregnancy or recent molar pregnancy. Others may be transient, such as obesity, very high blood pressure, and undiagnosed uterine bleeding. Some of the others, however, indicate that the woman should *never* take the pill at any stage of her life.

RELATIVE

Family history of cardiovascular disease.

Diabetes.

High blood pressure.

Heavy smoker.

Aged thirty-five to forty-five.

Long history of pill use (10 years or more).

Severe fluid retention (e.g. from kidney disease).

Obesity.

Scanty or absent periods (or history of).

Severe depression.

Use of drugs which interfere with the pill, or which the pill affects (e.g. some drugs used to treat TB and epilepsy).

Severe headaches.

Gallbladder disease.

Gilbert's disease.

Surgery or childbirth within the last four weeks.

Major injury, or large plaster cast, on calf of one or both legs.

History of weight gain on the pill.

Conditions likely to make the woman unreliable at taking the pill (e.g. mental retardation, alcoholism, major psychiatric problems, poor previous history of pill-taking).

Lactation.

Severe asthma.

Severe epilepsy.

Severe varicose veins or phlebitis (ordinary varicose veins should not need to prevent pill-taking).

Danger signs

Once the woman has been screened regarding the above contraindications and been found suitable for the pill, the chances of her developing any of the life-threatening conditions related to pill use are very small. However, all women given the pill should be taught the danger signs to watch out for, just in case. They are the following:

Severe pain in one calf, especially if accompanied by swelling.

Severe central or side chest pain.

Unexplained breathlessness.

Cough with bloodstained phlegm.

Severe abdominal pain.

Prolonged, severe, unusual headache, especially if this happens for the first time after starting the pill, or if it gets progressively worse each time, or if the headaches keep recurring.

Bad fainting attack or other collapse.

Sudden weakness or very marked numbness and tingling on one side of the body or face.

Sudden disturbance of the eyesight or speech.

Severe generalized skin rash.

Jaundice.

Sudden confinement to bed.

These signs are occasionally contracted to a mnemonic for easy memory-jogging; they spell out the word ACHES.

Abdominal pain (severe).

Chest pain (severe) or shortness of breath.

Headaches (severe).

Eye problems (blurred or lost vision).

Severe pain in calf or thigh.

Notice, however, that these do not cover all the danger signs in the longer list. If any of these warning signs occur, stop pill-taking immediately and contact a doctor.

Other considerations

Some drugs, especially some of those for treating tuberculosis and epilepsy, can interfere with the pill's functioning. In these cases, a higher dose pill or an alternative contraceptive may be necessary. Large doses of vitamin C (e.g. 1g or more daily) can turn a low-dose pill into a high-dose one, so this kind of vitamin C intake is not recommended for women on the pill. With some drugs the opposite effect occurs; the pill can interfere with the other drug's efficacy. This can be true of some (not all) drugs taken for diabetes, anxiety, depression, high blood pressure and migraine. A few studies seem to show that pill-users may need to take in more vitamin B_6. This is still being investigated.

The pill should be stopped, if at all possible, at least six weeks before having major surgery, and also for at least four weeks afterwards. This will help to reduce the risk of clotting in the legs. Obviously pill use will not prevent you from having emergency surgery if this becomes necessary, but extra vigilance will be needed. If you know you are going to have an operation, prepare yourself beforehand with an alternative contraceptive. Incidentally, none of the rhythm methods is satisfactory as a back-up to pill-taking, as dates, temperature and mucus signs will all be inaccurate.

Women who have used the pill for several years can be tempted to blame the method if they later discover that they are infertile. It is *extremely* unlikely that their condition can be blamed on the pill. Remember that roughly 1 woman in 10 will have great difficulty conceiving in any case, and you are unlikely to discover this until you have stopped the pill and tried to conceive – then it can be all too easy to blame the pill. Similarly, if you have left it for a long time before starting to try for children (e.g. middle to late thirties), then your fertility will have declined because of your age, just as it does with women using other (or no) forms of contraception. The pill cannot restore you to a more fertile state than before you started it, any more than any other method of contraception can. On average, full fertility returns about three months later than if stopping other methods of contraception, but it may return immediately, even in the first few days of stopping the pill, especially if the woman is young – so be warned!

Many women are worried that if they conceive by accident while they are taking the pill, the baby will be damaged. There was some concern about this a few years ago when there seemed to be some evidence that such babies had a higher incidence of neural tube defects (such as spina bifida). In 1981 a WHO major report concluded that if there was any risk, it was so small as to be immeasurable. However, twins did seem to be more common among such pregnancies. To be on the safe side, most doctors recommend that you stop the pill three months before you want to conceive and use an alternative method of contraception. You should also stop taking the pill immediately if you become pregnant or suspect that you might be; it is never a good idea to subject a developing baby to unnecessary drugs. All the evidence currently available shows that there is no adverse effect on children of women who have used the pill in the past, although it does seem that in these cases twins may be less common.

Reliability
The combined pill is the most reliable form of reversible contraceptive, with a failure rate of 0.1-2 per 100 woman/years. Failures of the method are very rare indeed: failures caused by forgetting to take the pill account for far more of the unwanted pregnancies.

Advantages
The pill is an extremely effective method of preventing unwanted pregnancies. It is unrelated to sex, and so causes no interruption of lovemaking. It is very easy to use – simply swallowing a pill – and the regimes for ordinary pills are easy to follow. It is discreet to use and easy to carry around when travelling or holidaying. It is available free from GPs and family planning clinics. It appears to have no effect on subsequent pregnancies, even those conceived accidentally. The method is virtually one hundred per cent reversible. It helps protect against some forms of cancer and some other minor and major health conditions. It also improves and regulates the menstrual cycle and associated problems.

Disadvantages
The pill does carry a high risk for some women and is very occasionally a contributory factor in a woman's death. It can increase the incidence of quite a few major and minor diseases and medical conditions. It needs to be issued by a trained person, and cannot be bought over the counter. Not all women are suitable candidates for pill use. The pill interferes with the body's hormonal systems, and can delay the return of fertility for a few months.

Conclusions
If you are happy with the idea of hormonal contraception, then there are no ethical problems with the combined pill, but you must check very carefully that you are a suitable candidate. The ideal pill user is a normal-weight woman in her twenties who is conscientious about pill-taking, does not smoke, and has no health problems. If you are forgetful, over thirty-five, overweight, a smoker, or dislike taking medication of any sort then you will not be a good candidate for the pill. Because of the pill's excellent success rate it is a very good method for the first few months/years of marriage, especially where the woman is young and therefore very fertile. It causes very little embarrassment to use, and means that the couple should be free to discover one another sexually without the hindrance of mechanical methods, the abstinence of rhythm methods, or the fear of unplanned pregnancy. If you are concerned about the health risks, then you should weigh them up very carefully against how important it is to you not to become pregnant. The woman needs to be happy with taking charge of contraception – it is difficult for the man to participate in this method, other than by reminding his wife to take her pill. Lastly, every pill user (and her husband) should be aware of the danger signs.

MINI-PILLS

The mini-pill has been around in this country for over a decade. The name is slightly misleading; it is not a very low dosage of an ordinary combined contraceptive pill, as many people think. The mini-pill contains only progestogen, rather than progestogen and oestrogen; hence its other name of progestogen-only pill (POP). Even its dosage of progestogen is smaller than is usually found in combined pills.

Because the mini-pill contains no oestrogen, it is considered much safer than the combined pill for women at risk from the oestrogen-related side-effects especially those involving the cardiovascular system. It is also considered safer for women over thirty-five, and those with a history of bad headaches or high blood pressure.

How it works

The progestogen in the mini-pill has little effect on ovulation in some women. About forty per cent of those taking the mini-pill will still experience normal ovulation and periods. Twenty per cent more will vary between ovulatory and anovulatory cycles – those with and without an egg. The other forty per cent will rarely or never experience ovulation. In some women the dose of progestogen does suppress ovulation completely; in these cases the woman will not have any monthly bleeding. One of the main effects of the mini-pill is to make the cervical mucus thick and virtually impenetrable to sperm. It also acts on the lining of the uterus so that if an egg is fertilized it will not be able to implant.

Taking the pill

The mini-pill is taken every day, including during periods. It is important that this pill is taken at the same time every day, as its margin for error is much smaller than that of the combined pill. The ideal time to take it is in the early evening, at about six or seven p.m. This is because the pill exerts its maximum effect on the cervical mucus about four hours after it is taken. Since most couples generally make love late at night when they go to bed, this ensures that the maximum contraceptive effect occurs more or less at the same time as intercourse. This doesn't mean that you will get pregnant if you make love in the morning or at lunchtime, but it is best as a general rule. The worst time to take the mini-pill is last thing at night, as if you make love then you will be relying on the tail-end of the effect of the previous night's pill.

Because the dosage is so low, if you forget to take your pill within three hours of the normal time (or if your system is interrupted by vomiting or diarrhoea), you should continue to take the pills but use a back-up method of contraception for the next 14 days. Some doctors feel that this is over-cautious, and that 7 days would be enough, but until this is officially approved it is best to play safe.

When you start to use the mini-pill, you begin with the first pill on day 1 of your normal cycle – the first day of your period. From then on you take a pill every day for as long as you wish to use this method. For the first 14 days (again, some doctors say 7), while the hormone level builds up, you will need to use an alternative form of contraception. After that time you should be protected from conception all the time including during periods.

It is possible to start the mini-pill on the day of a miscarriage or abortion, again with 7 or 14 days of extra protection. After childbirth you can start the mini-pill on around day 7, and the contraceptive effect will be immediate. If you are breastfeeding, you can delay starting the pill until the fourth week. Incidentally, the mini-pill can be used during breastfeeding. Unlike the combined pill it has no effect on the quantity of the milk and very little on the quality. For all women taking the mini-pill, regularity and conscientiousness in pill-taking is very important. As Guillebaud says, 'this pill is not for the forgetful'.

Side-effects
The most common side-effects of the mini-pill relate to the

woman's periods. They may become irregular or shorter, disappear altogether, or spotting may occur between periods. If your periods disappear altogether, it probably means that you are very well-protected against pregnancy, as this implies that you are not ovulating. Of course it could also mean that you are pregnant, especially if this sign occurs suddenly after more normal periods on the mini-pill. Mini-pill users are generally told to expect irregularities in their periods – they may be as infrequent as one or two a year. Dysmenorrhoea (painful periods) can be reduced in some users, though not as much as in women who use the combined pill.

Other side-effects can include headache, raised blood pressure, hirsutism, dizziness, weight gain, liver problems, loss of libido, and breast tenderness. Again, these are less common than among combined-pill users. Unlike the ordinary pill, the mini-pill appears to increase the incidence of ovarian cysts. Contraindications against use of the mini-pill tend to be the same as against the combined pill (see p.69). Once again, doctors are probably being over-cautious, and some are more easy-going over these rules. Abnormal genital bleeding becomes a more important contraindication against the mini-pill than the combined pill, as the mini-pill itself can produce irregular bleeding. Also a past history of ectopic pregnancy militates against the use of the mini-pill, as pregnancies resulting from this pill failing are more likely than usual to be ectopic.

Diabetes (known or suspected) and acute mononucleosis (glandular fever) can also be contraindications. The danger signs for women on the mini-pill are the same as those for the combined pill (see p.67). The mini-pill does not have to be stopped before surgery or if the woman is immobilized, as it contains no oestrogen which is the danger factor in these cases.

Effectiveness
The failure rate of the mini-pill is somewhat higher than that of the combined pill, and varies between 0.5 and 4 per

100 woman/years. The lowest failure rate occurs among women who are thirty-five to forty, whose fertility level has declined already. Because the pill dosages are so low, missing one pill can quite easily lead to pregnancy. It is thought that fertility is re-established virtually immediately the mini-pill is stopped, although for those women who have actually stopped ovulating it may take a little time.

Conclusions
The mini-pill has many of the benefits of the combined pill (discreetness, portability, ease of use) without many of the combined pill's associated health risks. However, the mini-pill is slightly less reliable than the combined pill, and does carry an increased risk of ectopic pregnancy. The mini-pill is subject to the same ethical criteria on hormonal contraceptives as the combined pill, except that its method of working is different. Couples thinking about using the mini-pill instead of the less safe combined pill should think very carefully; they may be swopping greater risk to the woman for the risk of causing occasional early abortions. To maximize the actual *contraceptive* effect of the mini-pill, the woman should take it regularly in the early evening.

INJECTABLES
The two injectable contraceptives that to date have been tested fairly rigorously are depot medroxyprogesterone acetate (DMPA) and norethindrone enanthate (NET-EN). Both of these are progestogens, or progestins, and between them they are currently being used in eighty countries around the world.

DMPA
This drug is most commonly marketed under the brand name Depo-Provera. A similar drug was first synthesized in 1958, and used (unsuccessfully) to treat threatened miscarriage. It was soon discovered that large doses in injection form had a contraceptive effect. Like most other progestogen-only contraceptives, DMPA has several effects

which combine to prevent pregnancy. It works on the pituitary to inhibit the secretion of LH and FSH, which interrupts the chain reaction that leads to ovulation. It also acts on the tissues of the fallopian tubes, and on the cervical mucus to help prevent sperm penetration. In addition it atrophies the endometrium, which prevents implantation of any ovum that might be fertilized.

The drug is administered by injection, generally in a regime of 150mg every three months. The efficiency of this regime varies between 0-1.2 pregnancies per 100 woman/years. A less usual regime of 400-450mg every six months has a slightly higher pregnancy rate – up to 3.8 per 100 woman/years in one study. The drug has to be given within 5-7 days of the beginning of a period, otherwise the woman may already be pregnant. The drug actually gives more than three months' protection per 150mg, but is overlapped to prevent a sudden drop in blood levels and to give a little leeway in case the injection is delayed. One disadvantage of the method is that it cannot be reversed until that particular dose of the drug has worn off.

The most common side-effect is disturbance of the menstrual cycle. This can take the form of excessive bleeding or of absence of periods, which often disappear completely after 9-14 months on the drug. Of course for some women this is a boon rather than a disadvantage, but others may begin to fear that they are pregnant. Bleeding can be induced by giving oestrogen supplements, but this cancels out one of DMPA's main benefits – that it gives the security of a hormonal method without the health risks associated with oestrogen-containing pills. Other side effects can include headache, abdominal bloating, mood changes, decreased libido, dizziness, weight gain, depression, and allergic reactions. DMPA has very little effect on blood pressure.

DMPA does not inhibit lactation once breastfeeding is well established, and there is so far no evidence that it can harm a breastfed infant, although it does cross into the milk to some extent. It has been recommended by some bodies that it should not be given until at least six weeks after giving birth. Practitioners tend to use the same absolute contra-indications for DMPA as for the combined pill (see p.69), with the addition of undiagnosed uterine bleeding. So far, however, it has not been shown to increase the risk of any lethal conditions.

There has been a great deal of controversy over trials of the drug done on beagle bitches and monkeys, which seemed to imply that the drug might act as a catalyst for breast tumours or endometrial cancer. The beagle trial is now suspect as many medical bodies (including the UK Committee for the Safety of Medicines and the WHO) have concluded that beagles are not suitable models for predicting human reactions to the drug. Nevertheless, as a precaution, all DMPA users should practise conscientious breast self-examination.

The monkey trial also seems to have been a false alarm, partly because the two monkeys affected were on fifty times the human dose, and partly because the tumours appear to have arisen from a cell type not found in humans. Studies on other animals suggest that DMPA may harm a foetus conceived while using the drug. These results are still inconclusive.

One of the less desirable effects of DMPA is that it delays the return of fertility. The length of the delay is unpredict-able, but it is generally agreed to average about 7 months (some studies say 5.5, some say 10). By 12 months after stopping the drug, over 20% of women trying to conceive had still not done so – by 24 months the percen-tage was 7.9%. Infertility is still not considered a serious problem by many doctors working on the trials, although presumably some of the women concerned have a different opinion.

DMPA has been the centre of some controversy in this country, but has recently been given Department of Health approval for use by women who are unsuited to other methods. It has been used with considerable success in certain parts of the country. The WHO and IPPF (International Planned Parenthood Federation) are happy with DMPA on the present evidence, but the USA has not approved it yet; it feels that so far there is not sufficient evidence to say that the drug is harmless. Also some authorities are not happy about the potential hazards of the irregular bleeding problems it induces. If these could be conquered it would be more acceptable to both doctors and patients.

NET-EN

NET-EN is not as well-known as DMPA, and has not been so widely used and tested. Nevertheless many women have taken part in trials, and the drug so far has some attractive advantages over DMPA.

The standard dose is not quite so long-acting as DMPA. It has been suggested that it is administered every twelve instead of every thirteen weeks, but even this gives a rather too high pregnancy rate at the end of the injection interval. Some clinicians are working on a regime of 8-week intervals for 6 months, followed by 12-week intervals from then on; others prefer a standard 10-week interval. The four major trials have given pregnancy rates of 1.5-5.2 for 13-week intervals; most of these pregnancies occur in the third month of the first injection.

The drug seems to inhibit ovulation completely at the beginning of the interval, although there is some evidence that it can return during the third month. The cervical mucus is less hospitable to sperm, and some, but not all, studies show that the endometrium is affected so that it discourages implantation of a fertilized ovum.

Side-effects include possible menstrual disruption, mainly spotting, decreased flow or irregular periods. The two extremes of absence of periods and heavy bleeding are not so common with NET-EN as with DMPA, which may make NET-EN more acceptable to many women. Other side effects can include headache (fairly frequently), also anxiety, abdominal discomfort and loss of libido. There does seem to be a measurable weight gain for most women using NET-EN; also the drug seems to be stored better by overweight women than by underweight ones, who apparently run a higher risk of becoming pregnant! The drug also appears to help protect against the infection, vaginal moniliasis.

Fertility is re-established more quickly after NET-EN than after DMPA, with an average delay of 1-4 months. So far no abnormalities have been found in foetuses conceived accidentally while using NET-EN, but further research is needed before this can be stated definitely. The drug does not appear to have any effect on milk production during lactation, but some of the drug does cross into the milk.

Advantages of injectables
Injectables are very easy and reliable methods of contraception, although they do have some failures. Once the drug is administered, nothing more needs to be done until it is time for the next injection. As a result, there is little or no difference between the theoretical failure rate and the actual failure rate. As with other progestogen-only contraceptives, injectables avoid most of the serious complications associated with oestrogen-containing pills. Effectiveness often continues even when the next injection is a little late, and is good in all respects for forgetful women. The drugs do not appear to suppress lactation, and using a regime of injectables may decrease the incidence of anaemia through their interruption of the menstrual cycle.

Disadvantages
Injectable contraceptives cannot be reversed until the effect of the latest injection has worn off – this means that they are not under the full control of the user. Menstrual disruption is a common side-effect of the drugs, and the return of fertility can be delayed considerably after the drug is stopped. In common with other progestogen-only contraceptives, they may work partly by preventing implan-

82

tation of a fertilized ovum, which means that the Christian should consider very carefully before choosing this method of contraception using the above drugs. This method of contraception is only possible with medical supervision.

Conclusions

Injectable contraceptives as a theory have a promising future; for women who are happy with hormonal methods, these could provide very effective long-term protection with the minimum of participation and bother. In practice, neither of the two main injectables is trouble-free, and at the moment neither is generally available in this country.

IMPLANTS

Implants are small capsules which are placed under the woman's skin. They release hormones into the bloodstream which prevent pregnancy.

The main implant to have been tested to any extent is NORPLANT. These capsules release the progestogen, levonorgestrel. Under a local anaesthetic, six small capsules of sealed silastic tubing are placed in a fan shape under the skin on the woman's arm. The operation requires a 3 mm incision, and takes only five to ten minutes. Once in place, these capsules protect against pregnancy for at least five years; the failure rate is 0.5 per 100 woman/years. The capsules require no attention until the end of the five years, when they are removed; removal may take up to twenty minutes, depending on the amount of fibrous tissue that has grown around them. If the patient wants the contraceptive reversed before the five-year period is up, the capsules are simply removed early; fertility returns 'without delay', according to the reports published so far.

The capsules work like other progestogen-only contraceptives; they suppress ovulation in some cycles, thicken the cervical mucus to make it virtually impenetrable to sperm, and possibly alter the endometrium to prevent implantation. Because of this last factor, they should be subjected by the Christian to the same careful consideration as other progestogen-only contraceptives (see p. 55).

Disadvantages
The most common side-effect is menstrual disruption, which is the most frequent reason for discontinuing the method. The disruption may be heavy periods, prolonged periods, or spotting between periods. For ten per cent of women using NORPLANT, the average is 77 days of menstrual bleeding per year – about six days per period. This average does tend to decrease as the contraceptive is used for longer, so does not seem to lead to anaemia through excessive blood loss. Other reported side-effects can include headache (fairly frequent) and depression, loss of libido, irritability, loss of appetite, nervousness and dizziness (less frequently).

Through the five years of use, the dosage of progestogen is around 30mg per day – well below the level used in combined contraceptive pills, and more equivalent to the dosage of the mini-pill. However, recent research has suggested that the use of norgestrels such as levonorgestrel in progestogen-only contraceptives may in the long term contribute to problems of the cardiovascular system. Another area of concern is the suspected link between progestogen-only contraceptives and ectopic pregnancy; the Progestasert® IUD has been specifically linked with ectopic pregnancies by the USA's Federal Drugs Administration. Both of these areas of concern are still being investigated, and may turn out to be drawbacks of this method for some or all women.

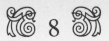

Rhythm methods

Rhythm methods are all based on the concept of avoiding sex during the most fertile part of a woman's monthly cycle. The original (calendar) method of birth control has been around for many years, and was pioneered to a large extent by the famous Marie Stopes. Unfortunately the contemporary understanding of the timing of the ovulatory cycle was very limited and often faulty, which presumably led to quite a few unwanted pregnancies!

However, it began the detailed investigations into the ovulatory cycle and ways of using this understanding as an aid to contraception. In the intervening years much progress has been made in ways of pinpointing the woman's most fertile time, including analysis of her temperature, blood hormone levels and cervical mucus, and also by recognizing other factors such as mid-pain, bleeding patterns, breast discomfort etc.

Meanwhile, first the mechanical and then the hormonal methods of birth control were receiving increased publicity, plausibility and use. Women began to feel that they at last had safe, reliable, trouble-free methods of contraception, which tended to make them turn away from the more complicated rhythm methods. This did not apply so much to Roman Catholics, as rhythm methods are still the only birth control methods sanctioned by the Catholic church. However, the last few years have seen many women turning back to rhythm methods, for several reasons.

First of all, many of the 'safer' methods have been in part discredited. IUDs are linked with increased incidence of pelvic inflammatory disease, ectopic pregnancies and perforation of the uterus, as well as being proved in some cases to prevent implantation of the fertilized egg rather than prevent fertilization. The pill has been linked with various minor and more serious side-effects, even death, in some users, and some women are now not recommended to take the pill because of certain pre-existing medical conditions.

Secondly, advances in some of the rhythm methods have made them, theoretically at least, more reliable. Thirdly, many women have reacted against using chemical, mechanical or hormonal methods of birth control, and are preferring to use a method which makes use of a woman's natural fertility cycle – hence the common name of 'natural family planning'. Fourthly, stress has rightly been laid recently on the importance of couples taking joint responsibility over such important decisions as family planning; rhythm methods require the full co-operation of both the man and the woman to be successful.

On the surface, today's rhythm methods can look like an ideal choice for the Christian couple. However, as with every other method of birth control, there are important ethical considerations to be taken into account. I feel that there are two serious ethical objections to the rhythm method, and several more minor considerations to be taken into account.

The first serious objection is that regular abstention from sex for contraceptive purposes militates against the biblical concept of sex within marriage. As we have seen in chapter one, the biblical idea of sex within marriage is that it is a beautiful gift to be enjoyed freely within marriage as a special expression of love, not just to create children. The New Testament details guidelines for giving oneself joyfully and unstintingly to one's partner, and mentions specifically that there is only one reason for sexual abstinence within marriage:

> The husband should fulfil his marital duty to his wife, and likewise the wife to her husband. The wife's body does not belong to her alone but also to her husband. In

the same way, the husband's body does not belong to him alone but also to his wife. Do not deprive each other except by mutual consent and for a time, so that you may devote yourselves to prayer. Then come together again so that Satan will not tempt you because of your lack of self-control (1 Cor. 7.3–5).

As Tim and Beverly La Haye say in *The Act of Marriage*: 'In this passage of Scripture, every husband and wife are absolutely commanded to do that which satisfies their marriage partner.' The Bible spells out that husbands and wives are *not* to abstain from sex except for a certain length of time for prayer; even then Paul makes sure that he enjoins them to 'come together again'. This injunction from the word of God makes it very hard to credit Ingrid Trobisch's remark in *The Joy of Being a Woman* that 'natural family planning corresponds to the Biblical image of man'.

The rhythm methods of birth control are often described as carrying no risk to woman or baby – this is untrue. The second serious objection to this type of contraception concerns babies conceived accidentally when using rhythm methods. There is some evidence that such babies may be more likely than usual to suffer defects of the central nervous system, and that the incidences of ectopic pregnancy (implantation in the fallopian tubes) and placenta praevia (misplacement of the placenta in the uterus) are also increased.

These occurrences are more common because the babies are generally conceived when either the sperm or the ovum is at the end of its natural life-span and beginning to decay; consequently in some cases the pregnancy does not proceed normally. This is an important consideration for women who object to the IUD or the pill because they can damage mother or baby – so can the rhythm methods. Ectopic pregnancy still carries a risk of death to the mother, and two ectopic pregnancies can leave a woman permanently sterile, as well, of course, as meaning that the baby's life cannot continue.

Other objections are less serious from an ethical point of view, but important nevertheless. One is the use of the word 'natural', as in 'natural family planning' or 'natural birth control'. Certainly the rhythm methods make use of the woman's natural cycle of fertile and infertile times – but there's nothing natural about taking your temperature early every morning, or abstaining from sex within marriage. Wendy Cooper in *The Fertile Years* says: 'It now seems absurd to insist that menstrual charts, basal temperatures, thermometers, and sex according to the calendar rather than desire, is somehow more natural than the pill which, after all, allows expression of natural feelings at a natural time.'

On this same point, Gavin Reid in *Starting Out Together* says: 'Quite honestly, this sort of view is emotional rather than intelligent. God has put us in a world where there is food to eat and where there are chemicals to be extracted which have properties we can discover and put to use. I call this "natural".'

Another objection to over-enthusiastic recommendation of rhythm methods is the emphasis that ardent proponents put on the value of abstinence. God does not require sexual abstinence from us in marriage; he has given us marriage so that we do not have to practise sexual abstinence, and in fact his word specifically teaches that we should not deny each other sexually within marriage. I'm not denying at all that the fellowship experienced by some couples in sharing this method of birth control can be valuable in deepening a relationship, but I do object strongly to the way that some enthusiasts seem to value abstinence more highly than sex:

'When we wanted a child, and therefore had intercourse more frequently, the experience became not quite as fulfilling. In times when we don't need the discipline [of absti-nence], as for instance during the time of pregnancy where there is neither menstruation or ovulation, it is almost as if something is lacking.' This is twisting out of recognition the picture of joyous, free, unstinting sexual fulfilment in marriage that the Bible gives. As Joyce Huggett says in *Growing Into Love*: 'This method of family planning concertinas the joys of sexual intimacy into a very limited space of time; a restriction which is to be questioned if we really believe that sexual intercourse is a major means of conveying a special sense of belonging.' She goes on to say: 'The safe period involves a calculated human intervention directed at avoiding conception as much as any other method, so why not allow couples to avail themselves of a choice of contraceptive?'

Tim and Beverly La Haye see the rhythm method as being a sensible way of calculating when you do and don't need to use other methods of contraception, and I would echo this view. To those who find barrier methods such as the sheath, cap or sponge a bit of a drag (and who doesn't?), then being aware of your own fertile times can limit the number of days in a month when you need to use these methods. I'm not suggesting that no Christians use the rhythm methods of birth control. If both partners are agreed that this is the method they choose, then fair enough – what I have done is to point out that there are major flaws in this method from the Christian point of view, as there are with most other methods. But to claim that this is the only 'Christian' method of birth control, as some people do, is indefensible.

Practicalities

The basic principle behind all rhythm methods is the same: to abstain from sex during the time in her monthly cycle that a woman is most likely to conceive (see p.21). Consequently, sperm and ovum never meet, and pregnancy will be avoided. There are various types of rhythm method which use different means of calculating the fertile time, with different degrees of success.

Several factors are relevant to all rhythm methods. The first is that women ovulate at only one time in their monthly cycle (occasionally two eggs are produced within twenty-four hours, which can lead to the conception of fraternal twins). As a result, sex should be safe after the ovum has had time to leave the body or has become 'over-ripe' and therefore impossible to fertilize. The second factor which needs to be built into the calculations is that ova can live for up to forty-eight hours before this point. The third factor is that sperm can survive for up to four days in the woman's reproductive tract if conditions are favourable.

CALENDAR METHOD

The oldest known rhythm method (indeed many people still believe that this is the only one) is the calendar method. This is also the least reliable of the rhythm methods. As its name implies it is based on the dates of the woman's menstrual cycle; a record needs to be kept for twelve months before you begin to use this method, to ascertain the pattern of your menstrual cycles.

On average, women ovulate 14 days before the beginning of each period; in practice it is more likely to be within two days either way, i.e. 16-12 days before a period. Since sperm can live for up to four days, then four days before the earliest possible time of ovulation are also unsafe – this gives a date of 20 days before a period. As an ovum can survive for up to forty-eight hours, then two days after the latest possible time of ovulation are also unsafe – this gives a date of 10 days before a period. If you have a perfectly regular 28-day cycle, from the chart on p.91 you can see that days 9-19 *inclusive* (this is important) are unsafe. If you have a regular 25-day cycle, days 6-16 inclusive are unsafe. For a 32-day cycle, days 13-23 are unsafe.

Most women's menstrual cycles are not the same length each month, which is why a twelve month record needs to be kept to make this method at all accurate. For instance, you may find that your shortest cycle is 25 days and your longest 30. Because it is impossible to predict at the beginning of a month whether this is going to be a long cycle or a short one, you need to build in extra precautions to cover

28–DAY CYCLE

1 2 3 4 5 6 7 8 9 10 11 12 13 14 15 16 17 18 19 20 21 22 23 24 25 26 27 28 1

lifespan of sperm - sex unsafe   ovulation sometime here   lifespan of ovum - sex unsafe   First day of period

25–DAY CYCLE

1 2 3 4 5 6 7 8 9 10 11 12 13 14 15 16 17 18 19 20 21 22 23 24 25 1

lifespan of sperm   ovulation sometime here   lifespan of ovum   First day of period

32–DAY CYCLE

1 2 3 4 5 6 7 8 9 10 11 12 13 14 15 16 17 18 19 20 21 22 23 24 25 26 27 28 29 30 31 32 1

lifespan of sperm   ovulation sometime here   lifespan of ovum   First day of period either eventuality. To find your earliest possible unsafe day you will need to take 20 days from your shortest ever cycle: this gives day 5. To find your latest possible unsafe day, you need to take 10 days from your longest ever cycle: this gives day 20. Therefore from day 5 to day 20 inclusive of every monthly cycle you will need to abstain from sex. That's over two weeks of every month! The calendar method combines the maximum amount of abstention for the minimum amount of reliability; if you want to use a rhythm method of birth control, you would do much better with one of the others.

TEMPERATURE METHOD

This rhythm method is based on the fact that a woman's basal body temperature (the temperature after rest) rises in the days immediately after ovulation. The rise can be as much as 1° F (0.6°C); in some women it may be much less, for instance 0.4°F (0.2°C). Most women also exhibit a drop in the BBT just before this rise, which can help pinpoint it. The rise occurs because of the rise in the body's progesterone level (see p.18) after ovulation.

Many women's temperature changes are not immediately obvious – especially as the temperature tends to fluctuate somewhat during other parts of the month – so records should be kept for at least six months before the method is used. By doing this you can train yourself (or be trained) to interpret your own personal temperature patterns. The temperature should be taken ideally at approximately the same time each morning, before 7.30a.m., and before getting out of bed, doing any activity at all, or taking any hot food or drink. It must be taken after at least one hour's complete rest; this means that if a woman has been up with fractious children in the night, she can still take an accurate temperature reading provided she has rested for at least an hour previously.

The temperature can be taken either orally, rectally or vaginally; rectally is most accurate. The temperature level is plotted in a special graph designed to show up small changes. The temperature rise needs to be sustained for twenty-four hours before it can be definitely attributed to ovulation, so two clear days should be left after the first rise before sex is safe – one day to ensure that ovulation has taken place, and one further day until the ovum's life-span is over. The evening of the third day should be safe.

Advantages and disadvantages

The temperature method is more accurate than the calendar method, since it is possible to pinpoint ovulation with some accuracy, but it has the same drawback that it cannot predict when ovulation will take place. As a result, sex has to be avoided for four days before the earliest possible time for ovulation – hence the need to keep records of previous cycles. Because of this uncertainty, the *Which? Guide to Birth Control* says: 'The temperature method on its own works best if you restrict sex to the second half of the cycle.'

Not all women experience a very sharp and sudden temperature rise. Some women's temperature patterns are step-like, zig-zag or 'double-shifted' (showing two peaks). Also, a woman doesn't always experience the same pattern of temperature rise each month. To complicate matters, the temperature can be affected by childbirth, abortion or miscarriage, activity before taking the temperature, high levels of alcohol in the blood, smoking a cigarette, physical or emotional upset, sleeplessness, stress, travel, and almost any illness – not just those producing high fevers. All of these factors can at times contribute to temperature charts that are confusing and difficult for the woman herself to interpret.

In addition, as Howard Shapiro says in *The Birth Control Book*, 'the burden of charting temperatures in the early morning when you are only half awake may lead to inaccuracies both in taking the temperature and in recording it.'

However, even if you are as heavy-lidded as an iguana early in the morning, all is not lost. There is one school of thought which says that you can choose instead to take your temperature either at 5p.m. or at bedtime each day, whichever fits best into your routine. If you take your temperature at 5p.m., it will consistently be approximately 0.7°F (0.39°C) higher than your morning BBT. If you take it at bedtime, it will only be approximately 0.3°F (0.17°C) higher. The temperature pattern over the month should echo that of your BBT.

This knowledge is also useful for occasional lapses in early morning temperature-taking. If things have gone wrong in the morning (for instance if you've overslept), you can take your temperature at 5p.m. and deduct 0.7°F (0.39°C) before plotting it on your chart, or you can take it at bedtime and deduct 0.3°F (0.17°C). As a rule it is not a good idea to mix the three timings – if you choose this method, stick to the same time each day as much as possible.

MUCUS METHOD

This method is based on the recognition of changes in the cervical mucus through a woman's menstrual cycle. It is often called the Billings method, after Drs E.L. and J.J. Billings who developed it fully.

Many women may already be aware that the mucus secreted in the vagina has different qualities at different times of the month, but may not realize that this is related to ovulation. From day one of the menstrual cycle the woman's oestrogen level slowly builds up to a peak at ovulation (see p.18); as the oestrogen level rises, the mucus secreted by the glands of the cervix changes in quality. From being scant and thick, creamy and opaque, it becomes clear, more liquid, very slippery and also stretchy. This provides an ideal medium for sperm to live in, and helps them travel easily through the cervix and on to fertilize an ovum. Gradually after ovulation, when progesterone is more dominant in the body, the mucus again becomes thick, sticky, opaque and impenetrable to sperm.

94

The essence of this technique is to recognize when the mucus is going through the changes which say that ovulation is imminent. The quality and quantity of the mucus can vary considerably from woman to woman and from one cycle to another, but the key factor is its stretchability. This is a quantifiable quality known as *spinnbarkeit* – 'that which can be drawn into a thread'. The *spinnbarkeit* reaches a peak around the time of ovulation, when the mucus can be stretched several centimetres; the mucus at this time is often likened to raw egg-white, very slippery and glassy.

If you rely on the mucus method alone, you should avoid sex from the time that the mucus begins to show *any* sign of clarity, wateriness, glassiness or *spinnbarkeit*. This involves checking the mucus several times every day, either by wiping the vulva with a tissue or toilet paper and then examining the mucus, or by doing a digital examination. Sex should be avoided until all trace of *spinnbarkeit* has disappeared for several days.

The mucus method has one advantage over the calendar and temperature methods: it can, in some women, give warning of ovulation. This is not always the case; as Shapiro says in *The Birth Control Book*, ovulation can occur one or two days before or after the so-called peak symptom (maximum *spinnbarkeit*). Without using any other methods to check when you have ovulated you will find it difficult to know which applies to you. For some women the time of ovulation can be obvious as they experience the *mittelschmerz* or midpain caused by congestion of the follicle (see p.18) when it is ready to burst. Women who don't naturally experience the *mittelschmerz* can provoke it by a rather bizarre method of bouncing up and down on a hard chair several times (see Shapiro), but I'm sure that this becomes rather tiresome!

If you are dedicated to using the mucus method to determine your fertile time, there are ways of improving or confirming your observations. One is by using a speculum (see p. 59) and mirror for self-examination; with this device you are able to see the external os (mouth of the womb). In this way, you can check whether there is little mucus, or whether it is dribbling, trickling or virtually pouring out of the os. The greater the quantity, the closer you are to ovulation, as a general rule. Also the os itself gradually opens towards the time of ovulation, and also lifts higher in the vagina. Both of these factors can help you slightly towards predicting ovulation, although they still might not give you enough warning to avoid sex – remember that sperm can live for up to four days.

Two other ways of testing the mucus can confirm the timing of ovulation. The concentration of glucose sugar in the mucus is high at the time of ovulation. In America kits have been developed to test and indicate the glucose level; these are not available in this country, but a similar test can be made by using diabetic Tes-tape. A short length of this can be secured over the tip of the finger with an elastic band, and the fingertip touched against the os. The yellow paper will turn various shades of green/blue towards ovulation, and dark blue when ovulation is imminent or has just taken place. Most proponents of the mucus method in this country prefer to train women to recognize the natural qualities of the mucus rather than to rely on testing kits.

A further method of testing the mucus is by microscope. Mucus smears taken at the time of ovulation show a phenomenon known as 'ferning' under a microscope – the specimen is made up of many branching arms like a fern. This ferning builds up to ovulation time, and disappears completely within two or three days. However, any traces of blood in the mucus negate this effect, and some women experience a very slight bleeding at the time of ovulation.

All of the methods used to check the cervical mucus can be adversely affected by infections of the vaginal area such as thrush or cervicitis. If you wish to use this method of birth control, it is advisable to have a thorough pelvic examination to check for any pre-existing infection before you begin charting your mucus pattern. The use of vaginal sprays and douches, which is not recommended by doctors in any case, can also disguise the natural character of the mucus.

SYMPTO-THERMAL METHOD

This is the most accurate of the rhythm methods; as the name implies it combines the temperature and the mucus methods. This means that the user gains the benefits of each; ideally she can recognize when ovulation is approaching by observing changes in her mucus and external os, and can also determine that ovulation has taken place by taking her temperature. This also means combining the disciplines of both methods; she must take her BBT every day, and also examine her mucus several times every day for the unsafe period.

For accuracy in interpretation, the temperature must be charted along with the quality, quantity and appearance of the vaginal mucus, position and appearance of the external os, midpain, spotting (slight bleeding at the time of ovulation), and menstrual bleeding. The greater the woman's diligence in observing and plotting these factors accurately, the safer the method.

Reliability

Of all the methods of contraception, the rhythm methods suffer most from the discrepancy between the theoretical failure rate and the actual failure rate (see p.24). This is directly related to the complexity of the method. If a woman just has to take a pill every day and nothing else she is fairly unlikely to get the process wrong (although it does happen), but the more detail and interpretation that is necessary for a contraceptive method the more chance there is for human error. This can work against the efficiency of the rhythm methods.

Ironically it is the mucus method, theoretically the most accurate of the three basic rhythm methods, which has the greatest discrepancy between theoretical rate and actual rate, because it is more complex and women find it more difficult to interpret the signs. Although the theoretical failure rate is only 2 per 100 women in a year, the actual failure rate is 25 – one in four women become pregnant over a year. The calendar method, which is known to be hit-and-miss, has a theoretical failure rate of 13 per 100 women in a year; in fact the actual rate is 21 – lower than that of the mucus method! The temperature method has a theoretical failure rate of 7 per 100 women in a year, with an actual rate of 20 – making all three methods much of a muchness.

The sympto-thermal method poses some controversy over failure rates. When Ingrid Trobisch's book *The Joy of Being a Woman* was published it gave this method's failure rate as up to 0.7% – less than it gave to the pill! This seems optimistic by any standards. In *An Experience of Love*, in answer to a charge of exaggeration on this point, Dr Roetzer (who pioneered this method) remarks that he feels this is accurate provided that all the detailed principles he lays down are observed. These take the form of rules regarding where the temperature rise occurs, its extent, and its relationship to changes in the cervical mucus. *The Which? Guide to Birth Control* states that: 'The most reliable study comparing the cervical mucus method with the sympto-thermal method suggested very little difference in pregnancy rates, which were around 20-24 per 100 women in a year.' It then goes on to say that 'some very enthusiastic users claim much better results'.

There is certainly an enormous discrepancy in these suggested failure rates, but one conclusion does seem to arise from all the discussions of the sympto-thermal method. Basically, the more dedicated you are to the method and the more conscientious your observations, then the lower your chances of becoming pregnant.

Advantages and disadvantages
All rhythm methods have several advantages in common. None of them uses anything hormonal or chemical, and

none of them uses anything mechanical at the time of intercourse. Both partners can be fully involved in implementing the method together, and for some couples this can lead to a deepening of their commitment. No previous preparations are needed for sex on the 'safe' days, and some couples also find that the 'unsafe' times encourage them to develop other ways of showing their love for one another. No medical complications or side effects occur to either partner except in some cases of accidental pregnancy. Used rigorously, the sympto-thermal method in particular has an acceptably high theoretical success rate. There are no problems with re-establishing fertility after using this method.

Some of the disadvantages are also common to all the methods. The woman's cycles have to be plotted for at least six months before the method begins (a year for the calendar method) so that she can learn to interpret them correctly. The most obvious disadvantage is that the couple have to abstain from sex for a certain time every month, which can be more than a fortnight in some cases. The longest periods of abstention are required by the calendar method. Some couples, or individual partners, find the required abstention ethically, emotionally or practically undesirable or unacceptable. All of the methods can be upset by illness, tiredness or stress. None of the methods is good for couples where one partner is away for long periods, for instance in the forces, as they may find that the time when they are together is 'unsafe'. The main potential risks of the method occur with unplanned pregnancies, where in some cases the pregnancy can be endangered or the child damaged.

Conclusions
It is often easy to say definitely that ovulation has taken place in a woman's menstrual cycle. The more factors that are observed, the more definitely this can be said, taking into account midpain, mucus changes, alterations in the position and appearance of the external os, temperature

changes, and spotting. It is then easy to avoid sex for a few days. What is not so easy is predicting when ovulation is going to take place, and avoiding sex for four days before that time. Research in rhythm methods (see p.141) is constantly trying to find a way of predicting ovulation; if this can be found, the time of abstinence would be reduced and might make the rhythm methods more acceptable and more accurate for more couples.

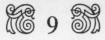

9

Intra-uterine devices

IUDS (intra-uterine devices, or coils, also known as IUCDS or intra-uterine contraceptive devices) are small pieces of plastic, or plastic and metal, which are worn inside the woman's uterus to protect against pregnancy. At first sight IUDS seem like ideal contraceptives. They can be worn for a long time, some even for many years, with only minimal routine checks. They have an acceptably high success rate. Their use is unrelated to the sexual act, and requires the minimum of participation from the user. Also, the method is easily reversible simply by removing the device. In practice, IUDS fall rather short of that ideal. Not only are they associated with some undesirable health risks, but their method of working poses problems for Christians.

When IUDS first became popular, little was understood about the way in which they protected from pregnancy. Research over recent years has shown that they work always or usually by preventing the fertilized ovum from implanting in the uterus (see p.23). In some way the presence of a foreign body in the uterus sets up an inflammation in the lining of the uterus and makes it hostile, instead of receptive, to the blastocyst (fertilized ovum). As a result, the blastocyst passes out of the body and the uterus lining is shed in the normal way as a period.

To those who believe that life begins at conception, this poses an enormous dilemma. By allowing an egg to be fertilized and then preventing it from implanting the IUD is causing an early abortion. Because the IUD does not generally prevent the egg from being fertilized, it should not be called a method of contraception – conception often still takes place. This fact tends to be omitted from many discussions of contraceptive methods both in books and from family planning practitioners. Drs Stanway, Stanway and Cauthery, (at least two of whom are Christians), in *The Complete Book of Love and Sex*, are some of the very few who actually point out that the IUD works in this way: 'It should be considered as a kind of extremely early method of abortion rather than a type of contraception.' Many women (and men), Christian and non-Christian alike, are ignorant of the way in which the IUD works. When a doctor or book tells them that IUDs are contraceptives, they accept this unquestioningly. It doesn't occur to them to ask *how* it prevents pregnancy, and many doctors are not concerned to tell them.

But does life really begin at conception? I believe that medical and biblical evidence proves that it does. On the medical front, it is well-known now that the fertilized egg contains the entire genetic blue-print that will determine that individual's unique characteristics. On the biblical front, Scripture makes it quite clear in several references that God is interested and involved in the child in the womb long before birth. When Mary (probably already pregnant) went to visit the pregnant Elizabeth, Mary could only have been a week or two pregnant. Yet the child in Elizabeth's womb (John the Baptist) recognized Mary, and possibly the child in Mary's womb (Jesus); he leapt with joy inside Elizabeth. If Mary had already conceived at this stage this is double evidence that there is something special about the unborn child, who in Mary's case was only days rather than months old.

Some people argue that in any case there is a high proportion of 'natural wastage' among fertilized eggs; many never implant successfully, or at all, and so are flushed out of the body anyway. It used to be thought that anything up to seventy per cent of all fertilized ova suffered this fate, but a recent study demonstrates that it is far fewer, maybe as few as eight per cent. Consequently we can have no precedent from nature, or God's plan, to treat a new life casually. As Dr Richard Winter points out, deliberately destroying a fertilized egg which may or may not be destroyed by natural processes is rather like the moral difference between falling under a bus and being pushed.

So, where does that leave the concerned Christian? My own view is, as far away from an IUD as possible. Dr Huw Morgan writing on medical ethics in the *Evangelical Times* raises the question of whether the IUD is a 'morally justifiable method of contraception'. Richard Winter points out that 'Once the IUD and post-coital pill are accepted there is little impetus in research to find more morally acceptable and reliable methods.' Tim and Beverly La Haye in *The Act of Marriage* say 'since it is an abortive device we DO NOT recommend it'. I feel just the same way. It may be that the progestogen-elaborating IUD has a slightly more genuine contraceptive effect if it does all the other things that other progestogen-only methods do, but even so the possibility of preventing implantation still occurs (see p.55). However, there does appear to be one exception to the normal IUDs and the way they work – see p.142 in the chapter on new developments.

The development of IUDs

It is often quoted in manuals of contraception that the forerunners of IUDs were stones that nomads used to put in the uteri of their camels to stop them becoming pregnant. The first known attempt to create an intra-uterine contraceptive device for humans was described in 1909. The device was a loop of thread made from silkworm gut. Later the Grafenberg ring of silver was developed in Germany, and the Ota ring of gold-plated silver in Japan. These were used by some practitioners up to the mid 1930s, when medical opinion rather turned against them. One doctor persevered with IUDs in Israel from 1930-57; he reported a failure rate of 2.5 per 100 woman/years. Interest reawakened in the late 1950s, perhaps as a result of this study; in particular the

USA became interested, and popularized several versions in the 1960s.

Progress was helped by the development in the 1960s of biologically safe plastics. This enabled manufacturers to produce IUDs which were pliable, and so could move with the changing shape and size of the uterus through the month, rather than digging in as the rigid metal IUDs did. The pliability also meant that the plastic had a 'memory'; the IUD could be forced into a narrow applicator for insertion, and would then resume its original shape when it was released in the uterus. Using a narrow tube as an applicator reduced the amount that the cervix needed to be dilated at fitting, which made the process quicker, safer and less painful.

In the late 1960s researchers began to experiment with IUDs wrapped in copper wire. This greatly increased the birth control effect of the device, but the IUDs needed to be changed more frequently. Recently an IUD has been developed which slowly releases progestogen. This too seems to add to the device's effectiveness. The IUD has always been more popular in some countries than in others. At present there are roughly 60 million IUD-users worldwide, including many in China. In the UK, approximately 4-6% of fertile women are IUD users.

Types of IUD
Many designs of IUD have been tried in different countries over the years. Some have never reached widespread production; others have been used and later withdrawn from the market for reasons such as increased risk of infection or septic miscarriage. The most commonly-approved IUDs are the Lippes Loop (one of the earliest types, and still used by more women worldwide than any other type), the Saf-T-Coil, the Copper-T, the Copper-7, and the Progestasert-T. The Copper-T and Copper-7, as their names imply, are IUDs which have wrappings of copper wire. The Progestasert-T is a progestogen-elaborating IUD. All the above

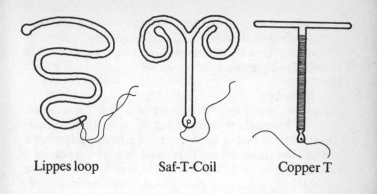

Lippes loop   Saf-T-Coil   Copper T

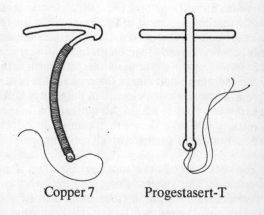

Copper 7   Progestasert-T

Types of IUD

styles are fitted with threads that hang down through the cervical canal and into the vagina. These help to reassure the woman that the IUD is still correctly in place, and also facilitates removal of the IUD if necessary. Generally practitioners prefer to use IUDs with tails, except in China where a particular tail-less model is popular.

How it works

For some years there was doubt as to just how an IUD worked. Researchers soon began to agree on one main effect, which is that in some way the IUD prevents implantation of a fertilized ovum. This could happen because of a local inflammation of the uterus; because of localized hormonal changes; because of a chemical imbalance affecting the endometrium; because of disruption of the normal hormonal pattern needed to sustain pregnancy; or because of mechanical disruption of the implanted blastocyst. It is also possible that the transport of the ovum down the fallopian tube may be accelerated, so that the blastocyst reaches the uterus before it is ready to implant. In addition it is possible that in some way the IUD immobilizes the sperm as they pass through the uterus and makes them incapable of fertilizing an ovum. However the incidence of pregnancy and ectopic pregnancy in IUD users makes this unlikely, as do recent animal tests which have shown that animals fitted with IUDs conceive numerous foetuses which can then be flushed out of their uteri.

It also seems certain that IUDs have no effect whatsoever on ovulation. The generally-accepted explanation for the IUD's effect is that it stimulates an inflammatory reaction in the uterus, which prevents the fertilized egg from implanting. This inflammation is sterile, that is, it is not associated with bacteria or viruses. Copper seems to stimulate this reaction, which explains the greater effectiveness of the IUDs which contain copper.

106

Suitability

Before being fitted with an IUD, various checks will be made. Details are taken of the woman's menstrual history (e.g. whether her periods are light, heavy, irregular, painful) and also of her fertility history (whether she has ever had a child, an abortion, a miscarriage, an ectopic pregnancy). She will also be asked whether she has ever had pelvic inflammatory disease (PID), if she has a history of IUD expulsion, and whether she intends ever to have any (more) children.

IUDs cannot be used in women with very small uteri, and women with an allergy to copper cannot use the Copper-T or Copper-7. Damage to the uterus or cervix during a previous childbirth may make an IUD undesirable. Also, some doctors prefer not to fit IUDs in women who have had caesarians, as there may be a likelihood of the IUD perforating the uterus through the old scar; other doctors are happy to fit IUDs to those patients provided at least three months have passed since the operation. IUDs should not be fitted if there is undiagnosed irregular bleeding, a history of PID, or large numbers of fibroids – these can alter the contours of the uterus and make the IUD ineffective. Some doctors prefer not to fit IUDs to women on anticoagulant or steroid therapy, or women with chest disease, some heart conditions, or renal disease. Any patient with anaemia should be treated before fitting, as most IUDs increase menstrual flow.

There is some disagreement over whether IUDs should be fitted in women who have never had children. The general consensus in this country is that they should not, as fitting is more difficult and there is an increased risk of PID with IUDs, which can cause future infertility. Other countries, and some individual clinics in this country, are prepared to fit IUDs in women who have never had children.

Fitting

Insertion of an IUD should always be done by a trained practitioner, either a doctor or a paramedical person fully trained in IUD fitting. Successful fitting of an IUD generally depends on whether the woman is relaxed, whether the correct size of IUD has been chosen, and the skill and experience of the practitioner. Insertion can be done at any stage of the menstrual cycle, but is preferable during or just after a period. This makes insertion easier, as the cervix is softer and more open, and also there is very little chance that the woman may be pregnant. However, the incidence of expulsion is also a little higher at this time. IUDs can be fitted immediately after childbirth, miscarriage or abortion, but then too the expulsion rate is higher; the optimum time if an IUD is to be fitted straight away seems to be about four days after the pregnancy has ended. Most practitioners prefer to wait until about six weeks after the birth.

The practitioner inserts a speculum, and examines the cervix and vagina to check that they are healthy. If the internal os is abnormal or damaged there is a high risk of IUD expulsion; if there is a cervical erosion, it is preferable to treat this before an IUD is fitted. A Pap smear may be taken at this stage. The woman is given a pelvic examination to check that her reproductive organs are normal and healthy. If the uterus is retroverted or acutely flexed this can make the fitting difficult.

The cervix is cleaned with antiseptic, and a local anaesthetic may be given if the woman is very tense or if the doctor will need to manipulate the uterus or cervix a great deal. A sound is inserted to check the length of the uterus. The chosen (sterile) IUD is fitted into a narrow tube, and the tube is inserted through the cervical canal. The IUD is released into the uterine cavity, and the tube withdrawn so that the IUD strings trail down through the cervical canal into the vagina. The strings are trimmed to about 3-5cm.

During fitting about 1 in 1000 women will collapse with so-called 'cervical shock'; IUD fitting rooms should always be equipped to cope with this kind of attack. Epileptics may run the risk of having an attack at the time of insertion, and the practitioner should be aware of this risk. Many women may experience backache or cramping discomfort soon after fitting; this can generally be relieved with ordinary analgesics. Some women may expel the IUD almost immediately, and others within the first couple of days; the woman should return to the clinic if bleeding or pain continues for more than a day or two.

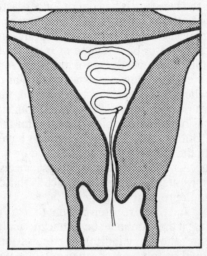

Lippes loop in position in the uterus

IUD users will be taught how to check with the fingers that the strings are in place. This should be done after every period, at mid-cycle, and after sex. The effectiveness of the IUD begins immediately, so no back-up method is necessary. The woman should attend all follow-up appointments, and any appointments to have the IUD replaced if necessary.

Side-effects

Bleeding problems are a common side-effect of IUD use. The Progestasert is the only IUD that is not known to cause heavier bleeding than the woman normally experiences – in fact this particular IUD may actually lessen bleeding. Up to fifteen per cent of users ask for removal of their IUD because of bleeding or spotting. Increased menstrual bleeding can mean that the bleeding is heavier or longer-lasting or both, sometimes to the point of pallor, weakness and anaemia. Bleeding may also be a sign of partial expulsion of the IUD. Some doctors prescribe a regime of iron supplements for three months out of every year for IUD users. A greater and/or longer menstrual flow can cause particular problems in cultures where there are restrictions on the woman's activities during menstruation; women from such cultures may be considered unsuitable candidates for the IUD. Various drug, vitamin and calcium treatments have been tried to alleviate the bleeding problems caused by IUDs, without notable success. Also, the use of drugs cancels out one of the main advantages of the IUD, which is that the method doesn't require regular drug use.

Cramping and pain are often present to some extent after an IUD fitting; if they continue, begin unexpectedly or become more intense, they may indicate a more serious problem. The IUD could be too large, or may not have unfolded correctly in the uterus, or the uterus may be expelling the device. Up to twenty per cent of users spontaneously expel the IUD within the first year, and many do not realize that they have done so. The percentage of expulsions varies with the type of IUD, the characteristics of the woman (e.g. her age), and the skill of the fitter. The danger of expulsion is greater during periods, as the cervix is more relaxed; also, the expulsion of the IUD from the body may be disguised by the menstrual flow. Symptoms of expulsion can include lengthening or disappearance of the IUD strings, post-coital bleeding, feeling the IUD at the cervix, and vaginal discharge. If not noticed, of course, expulsion may well result in a pregnancy.

Uterine perforation is a more severe side-effect of the IUD, and occurs in roughly 1 in every 2,500 insertions. The device may embed itself in the wall of the uterus, or perforate the cervix, or actually pierce the uterus. The Dalkon shield (now withdrawn from the market) was particularly associated with perforation. The Copper-T and the Lippes Loop seem to have low rates of perforation. The location of the IUD can be detected by ultrasound or X-ray; if it is badly displaced the woman may become pregnant.

Lost strings can cause concern to the IUD user, as she then can't tell whether her IUD is still in place. At times the strings can disappear up into the cervix or the uterus; if they are in the cervical canal they can often be retrieved, but if they have gone right up into the uterus this is more difficult. Special instrumetns have been devised to retrieve lost IUD strings, but it is generally better to remove the entire device and start again.

Pelvic inflammatory disease (PID) accounts for many of the hospitalizations (and some of the deaths) associated with IUD use. It is thought that perhaps the strings of the IUD encourage bacteria to travel up the cervix into the uterus, or perhaps that the already-inflamed lining of the uterus and the heavier blood flow act as culture mediums. The chance of contracting PID is considerably greater for IUD users than for other women. Unexplained or foul vaginal discharge is often the first sign of PID; other symptoms may be severe pain and cramping, and fever. PID can lead to endometritis, blockage of the fallopian tubes, peritonitis, abscesses and septicaemia, and can result in infertility. Women who have had previous incidents of PID are more likely to contract it again using an IUD, and many clinicians will not fit such women with an IUD unless they are sure that they don't want any (more) children.

Pregnancy
Pregnancy is possible with an IUD in place; it is also possible if the IUD has been expelled or has moved out of its proper

position. The chance of conceiving with an IUD still in place decreases as the woman's fertility declines. About 5% of the pregnancies which occur are ectopic, compared with 0.5% among pregnancies in non-IUD users. If the pregnancy is ectopic, then an immediate operation is necessary. Ectopic pregnancy can be a particular danger to an IUD user, as she may attribute the pain to her IUD and not get help quickly.

If the pregnancy has occurred with the IUD still in place, the IUD should be gently removed by the clinician, if possible within the first three months, if this is at all feasible. This removal will carry a 25-30% chance of precipitating a miscarriage (twice the normal rate in pregnancy). If the IUD cannot be removed and is left in place, there is a 50% chance of miscarrying the baby. Many of these miscarriages are likely to be 'septic' – associated with infection. Many of the deaths in IUD users are attributable to septic miscarriage or undiagnosed ectopic pregnancy. If the baby is carried to term safely, there is no evidence to suggest that it stands any more chance of being abnormal than babies of ordinary pregnancies.

Removal

IUDs may be removed for replacement, because the woman wants to get pregnant, or because she wishes to discontinue this method. Generally removal takes a few minutes, but occasionally there can be difficulties. Removal of the Copper-7 can be difficult because of its shape. Saf-T-Coils and Lippes Loops are generally removed fairly easily unless they have become embedded in the uterine wall. The pain on removal seems to be worse if the IUD has been in place for five years or more – it may have become embedded, or the cervical canal may have become narrower. Removal during a period is easiest as the cervix is more relaxed. Occasionally the doctor may need to anaesthetize the cervix and dilate it. IUDs containing copper should be replaced every 2-3 years, (apart from 5-year Novagen) the Progestasert-T every year, but the others can be left in place for much longer.

Other considerations
The return of fertility is an important area in relation to
IUDS, especially as PID and ectopic pregnancies can lead to
infertility. Roughly 85-90% of those discontinuing the IUD
because they want to become pregnant do so within a year
of removal. One advantage of the IUD is that it can be used
during breastfeeding, as it has no effect on lactation. The
safety record of the IUD outstrips that of the pill as the
woman gets older, her fertility declines, and the risks of the
pill become more dangerous. The IUD should always be
removed after the menopause.

Contraindications
There are some conditions which will prevent a doctor from
suggesting the IUD as a suitable method of birth control.
These are:

Pregnancy (known or suspected).

Acute or chronic (long lasting) pelvic infection.

Known or suspected malignancy of the cervix or uterus.

If the woman wants to have children in the future (this is
only true of some doctors).

Relative contraindications are those that the doctor consid-
ers may make an IUD inadvisable. These are:

Not having had children (not true of some doctors).

Painful periods.

Heavy periods or irregular bleeding.

Abnormalities of the uterus, e.g. double uterus, large
fibroids, very small uterus.

Lack of access to emergency treatment.

Multiple sexual partners (or history of).

History of pelvic infection.

Severe cervicitis.

Anaemia.

History of ectopic pregnancy

Some conditions such as renal disease, valvular heart disease, which would make an infection dangerous.

Being on anticoagulant therapy, or steroids.

Danger signs.
All women fitted with IUDs should be aware of the danger signs that can signal PID, pregnancy, miscarriage or an ectopic pregnancy. The initial letters spell out the mnemonic PAINS.

Period late or absent.
Abdominal pain.
Increased temperature, fever, chills.
Noticeable or foul discharge.
Spotting, bleeding, heavy periods, clots.

Reliability
The actual failure rate of the IUD is very close to the theoretical, as the woman has to do very little to continue using the method once the device is fitted. The theoretical failure rate is 1-3 per 100 woman/years (there is a slight variation among different styles of IUD). The actual failure rate is 4-10 per 100 woman/years.

Conclusions
The IUD is a long-acting method of birth control which generally needs little attention from the user. It has a high success rate, is discreet to use, does not alter the body's natural rhythms, and can be used by breastfeeding mothers. It is not suitable for all women, and is associated with several undesirable and a few fatal complications. Its chief drawback, however, which outweighs all other benefits and drawbacks, is that it generally acts by preventing implantation rather than preventing conception, which makes it morally unacceptable to those who believe that life begins at conception. For the exception to this method of action, see p. 142.

🏵 10 🏵

Postcoital Methods

Postcoital methods of birth control are those that are applied after sex has taken place. These methods assume that conception has, or may have, occurred – in the case of abortion, of course, it definitely has. Many people feel that using post-coital pills, IUD or menstrual extraction 'avoids' the moral dilemma of facing an abortion later. But using one of these methods in the hope of discontinuing any pregnancy that might have occurred is morally just the same as using one *knowing* a pregnancy has occurred – New Testament teaching makes it quite clear that intention as well as deed can be sinful. On most occasions when postcoital birth control is used, the woman has had sex unprotected by any form of contraception, although in some cases of abortion contraception has been used and has failed. Postcoital pills and IUDs are generally used as emergency methods of birth control.

In the past, methods used to try and prevent pregnancy from occurring after unprotected sex have included inserting pepper, cabbage blossoms or seeds into the vagina. Postcoital methods do not describe methods such as the normal IUD, which has its effect after conception has occurred but which is not applied to the body after conception. The post-coital IUD is one that is inserted into the woman after an episode of unprotected sex.

Because these methods assume that conception has taken place, once again moral and ethical problems are encountered. The postcoital pill and postcoital IUD are intended to work by preventing implantation of the fertilized ovum, and so for these methods the moral dilemma is the same as that over the normal IUD (see p.101). If you believe that life begins at conception, then preventing implantation is morally equivalent to inducing a very early abortion. Menstrual extraction is indeed a very early abortion if conception has taken place, and abortion itself of course involves ending the pregnancy early so that the embryo or foetus dies.

It is legally possible in this country for virtually any woman to obtain an abortion in early pregnancy if she is persistent. Whether abortion is legal or not has little to do with whether it is right or not. Once again I would stress that here I am not dealing with abortion of a handicapped child, or a child conceived illegitimately, adulterously, or as a result of rape – these cases have further ethical and spiritual considerations which are not part of this book. Here we are talking about a normal child which has been conceived accidentally within a normal Christian marriage; the parents either did not plan this child at all, or they did not plan one so early. What are they to do?

The first thing, in fact the vital thing, to remember is that although they did not plan this child, God obviously did. If the parents had sex without contraception, then they took a risk of pregnancy through their own choice; if the risk results in pregnancy then they cannot as responsible adults back out of that situation. As adults we are responsible for the consequences of our own actions, and if irresponsibility has led to a pregnancy, then the couple must accept that and do their best to redeem the situation and come to accept that child with love and joy. They have an extra, not a lesser, responsibility to love and care for that child because they brought about its birth by mistake; the child will probably already have to bear the burden of arriving at an inconvenient time of marriage or when there is little money around. Certainly abortion would solve one problem, but it will create a great many more.

What if the couple were using contraception, and then this failed? This gives them even more reason to see that

God intended them to have this child, as he overruled their human wisdom in using contraception by allowing them to conceive anyway. It is easy to become bitter at God when you are doing your best to be responsible and avoid pregnancy, and yet one occurs despite your efforts. This doesn't give us licence to halt that baby's life, however, just because we didn't plan it. God has often provided parents with an extra-special blessing through children who have been conceived in this way.

As Christians, we must never forget that God is the giver of *all* life – whether we plan it or not. No child is ever unwanted or unplanned to God, and our standards should be the same. God has a plan for that child's life just as he has for our lives, just as he has for the lives of children whose arrivals are planned by their parents. Charles Swindoll, the American pastor whose writings and teachings have inspired hundreds of thousands of Christians, was an 'unplanned' child. His parents didn't plan him, but God did – in fact, God planned something extra-ordinary for his life and ministry.

The Bible has an extremely high view of human life, and so should we have as Christians. I don't believe that anything in the Bible gives us a precedent for taking the life of an unborn child, especially not the life of a normal child conceived by a normal husband and wife within marriage. The answer to a trivializing view of human life is not to abort the unwanted babies but to want the ones that are conceived.

In any case, it is unlikely that even on the human level any baby is fully unwanted. Certainly, its parents may genuinely not want it or feel that they simply cannot cope, no matter how much support they are given. However, in this country alone there are literally hundreds of thousands of childless couples wanting to adopt children. Most of these couples will never be able to adopt even one child, there are so few available for adoption, yet most of them would happily adopt two, three, four or more children if they had the chance. All of these couples would need to be supplied with their full desired complement of children before we could ever say genuinely that a child was unwanted.

I don't want to make light of the enormous strains that an unplanned pregnancy can put on a marriage. Some couples cope very well with an early or 'surprise' child, and accept it into the marriage with little problem after the initial shock. On other couples it can impose a severe burden physically, financially or psychologically, especially if a child arrives before a marriage is fully established, or if there are already quite a few children in the family. It is no use saying that abortion is not an option for the Christian unless we provide alternative support – again, practical, financial and psychological – wherever it is needed. An unplanned baby is a shock to any marriage, but it is not a surprise to God; he began that life, and will give all the help necessary to sustain it if we as Christians appeal to him. I cannot believe that it can ever be his will to terminate a pregnancy simply because it was unplanned by the parents.

POSTCOITAL PILLS

Postcoital pills are hormones administered after unprotected sex; they are intended to prevent implantation from taking place if an egg has been fertilized. Of course at this stage it is too early to tell easily whether conception has occurred, so in some cases the pills will not be terminating a pregnancy at all; nevertheless, they are given with that intention.

The most common hormone used is a brand of the ordinary combined contraceptive pill; this has the fewest side-effects. Two tablets are taken within 72 hours of sex, and two more 12 hours later. This treatment may produce nausea, and even vomiting. The woman is warned to watch out for all the pill warning signs (see p. 71), although these are very unlikely to occur with this one-off dose. This treatment has a 0-1.6% failure rate; as yet there is no evidence of any harm to any baby which survives the treatment. High-dose progestogens are also used sometimes in the same way, but these are less common.

POSTCOITAL IUD

This treatment consists of inserting a copper-bearing IUD into the woman's uterus within five days of unprotected sex; it works by preventing implantation if an egg has been fertilized. As with the postcoital pill, the woman may not have conceived at all, but if she has the IUD will interrupt the progress of the pregnancy. This method has the 'advantage' that the IUD can be left in place and will prevent further pregnancies from continuing in the same way (see p.106).

MENSTRUAL EXTRACTION

This process is also known as menstrual regulation, and involves sucking out the contents of the uterus at the normal time for a period. Menstrual extraction first became popular among women's self help groups in the USA; it was evolved as a way of minimizing the discomfort and inconvenience of normal periods. A simple vacuum instrument is inserted into the uterus through the cervix, and the thickened lining of the uterus, which has begun to break down as a normal period, is extracted. In this way the menstrual bleeding that normally takes four to six days can be over in about half an hour; the process can be done by another woman, who does not need to be medically trained (at least in theory) – this is what has made it so popular with women's groups. Of course, if the woman is pregnant, the process also removes the young embryo at the same time and stops the pregnancy.

Although menstrual extraction was not developed as a form of birth control it can obviously act as one, and in fact the main interest in it these days is as a way of interrupting pregnancy. Medical opinion has advised that it is not a good idea to use it regularly simply as a means of making menstruation easier; it involves inserting a foreign body into the sterile environment of the uterus every month, which can lead to complications or infection. Many women feel that menstrual extraction every month would avoid the moral dilemma of choosing an abortion specifically, as each month they would not know whether they were pregnant or not. In fact, of course, the intention is still to abort any embryo that might be present in the uterus; Hatcher *et al.* in *Contraceptive Technology* actually advise that it is 'usually better to wait until a positive diagnosis of pregnancy can be made' rather than to use menstrual extraction every month regardless. In this case there would be no doubt that there was a pregnancy, and the woman would be making a definite choice to abort it by having a menstrual extraction.

ABORTION

Abortion is the interruption of the normal process of pregnancy, by the death of the foetus before the twenty-eighth week. This can happen spontaneously; in everyday language a spontaneous abortion is usually called a miscarriage. Abortion here is used to mean deliberate termination of a pregnancy.

Methods

Abortion is now legal in many countries. There are many highly dangerous methods of inducing an abortion, but the procedures used in legal abortions are as surgically safe for the mother as possible. Legal methods are divided into medical methods and surgical methods.

Medical methods introduce a substance into the body to induce labour and thus end a pregnancy early. The most common substances used are prostaglandins, which can be introduced into the amniotic fluid or as a suppository in the vagina. Prostaglandins can lead to the delivery of a live foetus. Saline is another common abortifacient; some of the amniotic fluid is removed and replaced with saline. The salt water kills the foetus, but can cause some problems to the mother. Urea is a third substance which can be used as a medical method, but it is more effective when used in combination with prostaglandins.

Surgical methods include vacuum curettage, D and C (dilatation and curettage), D and E (dilatation and evacuation), hysterotomy, and hysterectomy. Vacuum curettage is done under a local anaesthetic. A vacuum curette (a long hollow medical instrument) is introduced into the uterus to suck out its contents, then a sharp curette removes any remaining material. This needs only a small dilatation of the cervix, and can be done up to thirteen weeks into pregnancy. A D and C abortion is an adaptation of a technique used to treat various gynaecological conditions. The contents of the uterus are scraped out with a sharp metal curette. This requires a larger dilatation than a vacuum curette, and may increase the pain and blood loss.

D and E is a combination of the first two methods, and is used especially in the 13-16 week period, although it can be done up to twenty weeks into pregnancy. The cervix needs to be dilated more than for a vacuum curettage, and because the foetus is bigger the surgeon may need a crushing instrument for the skull and a larger-bore vacuum curette. This procedure can be done with a local or a general anaesthetic.

A hysterotomy is a small caesarian section; it requires a general anaesthetic, and because it is abdominal surgery there is an increased convalescence time. This technique is rarely used. Hysterectomy is the surgical removal of the uterus; this would only be used for an abortion if there were also a vital medical condition (such as advanced cancer) which required immediate removal of the uterus as well as the foetus.

Complications

Medical complications of abortion are kept to a minimum if: the pregnancy is in the early stages; the woman is healthy; the abortionist is skilled; local anaesthesia rather than general is used; the reproductive system is normal; and complete follow-up is provided by the clinic and used by the woman. Also, the material removed from the uterus should be examined to make sure that the pregnancy is not ectopic or molar. The death rates for legal abortion vary by method, but average:

1 in 400,000 before 9 weeks.
1 in 100,000 from 9 to 12 weeks.
1 in 25,000 from 13 to 16 weeks.
1 in 10,000 after 16 weeks.

Other medical complications are mainly caused by infection, incomplete removal of the foetus and placenta, blood clots, continuing pregnancy, cervical or uterine trauma (shock), and bleeding.

Warning signs of infection include cramping, fever, pain, discharge, and pelvic discomfort. The infection may affect the endometrium, the fallopian tube(s) or the abdominal cavity, and may lead to infertility. Incomplete abortion and blood clots lead to severe cramping pains, but can be remedied by vacuum aspiration or D and C. 0.1–0.3% of women are still pregnant after the abortion. This may be because the foetus was missed, or because the pregnancy was ectopic, or because the woman was expecting twins and only one was aborted.

A woman is advised after an abortion not to use tampons, not to have sex or douche for a week, and to take her temperature twice a day for the first week to check for fever. If her temperature reaches 100°F or more, or if she experiences severe pain, a rash, or has very heavy bleeding for two days, or any bleeding for two weeks, she must see a doctor urgently. If she has no period for eight weeks, or if other symptoms of pregnancy persist, she may still be pregnant. In any case women are advised to go for a follow-up medical check two weeks after an abortion.

Research into long-term effects of abortion is inconclusive, but some conditions are known to be associated with abortion in some cases. These include subsequent infertil-

* stream of water to cleanse for medical purposes

ity, and miscarriage, premature delivery or low birth weight of subsequent babies. There are also potential psychological and emotional effects, particularly (but by no means exclusively) for the Christian, including guilt, shame, remorse, and psychological disturbance.

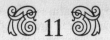

11

Sterilization

Sterilization is permanent contraception. Part of the reproductive system of either the man or the woman is removed or blocked so that the normal meetings of sperm and ova are prevented.

In modern history, sterilization has only been used as a method of contraception in recent years, but it was known in the ancient world. Ancient Egyptian authorities removed the ovaries of prostitutes, and in several cultures eunuchs who supervized harems or concubines were castrated – although this may have been to prevent sexual temptation rather than actual pregnancy. These methods are now considered too radical for practical use, as removing the ovaries or testes creates other side effects as well as producing sterility.

Female sterilization by cutting the fallopian tubes was suggested in medical literature as early as 1823, and in 1849 a technique of blocking the tubes with silver nitrate was described. In 1878 electric cautery of the tubes was suggested, and by 1880 an American surgeon had developed an effective operation which involved tying the tubes with silk thread. Different surgical methods continued to be developed and refined, until we reached the range of different techniques we have available today. So far, more than 100 million people worldwide have been sterilized. In the USA, more couples use sterilization than any other method of birth control. In the UK, roughly 35% of couples aged between thirty and forty-five have chosen sterilization.

Is sterilization an option for the Christian couple who do

not wish to have further children? Once again, opinions differ. Some people feel that it is not right for a couple to try to 'play God' and make sure that they never have any more children, as they feel that God might still have one or more planned for them. However, the reasoning behind sterilization is just the same as behind any other method of birth control; it is merely the time-scale that is different. If you plan not to have any more children and use another method of contraception for this reason, then your intentions are just the same as if you get sterilized, except that sterilization is probably safer and more reliable. As Saidi and Zainie say in *Female Sterilization*, 'the morality of voluntary sterilization seems no different than the morality of any other form of contraception'. If you as a couple feel that the principle of contraception is valid, and also believe before God that you do not feel he intends you to have any more children, then sterilization is a valid option.

One reason that people steer away from sterilization is that several incidents in history have given the concept unpleasant associations. One such incident began at the end of the last century, when certain prisoners in some USA states were forcibly sterilized to prevent them from passing on 'undesirable' characteristics. This practice was soon followed by many other countries, including our own. The other incident, of course, is the Nazi programme; in 1934 alone over 56,000 people were ordered to be sterilized, and similar programmes were carried out in the concentration camps. However, voluntary sterilization is a quite different matter, and many countries allow for this contraceptive option in their legislation. Sterilization is a very safe operation nowadays, both for men and for women, and the mortality and complication rate is very low. Nevertheless some risks do exist, as with most methods of birth control, and these should be weighed up when the option is being considered.

Sterilization is a very big step, and should never be undertaken lightly. Although there has been some small success in reversing sterilizations, and new research is constantly being undertaken with this aim in mind, success rates are very small indeed. For this reason, sterilization should *always* be considered permanent. This means that the person who is sterilized will never be able to father, or bear, a child again – and this is an enormous fact to be faced up to.

Sterilization should also always be the joint decision of both husband and wife. If one partner is, or appears to be, ambivalent, the wise doctor will refuse or delay sterilization. The couple also needs to be very clear exactly why they want to be sterilized. Reasons which are generally accepted as valid are that the couple have already reached the desired number of children; further pregnancy would be dangerous; couples don't feel that they can trust, or don't like, the reversible methods; or couples feel they cannot afford more children. Some clinics will also sterilize some couples who have decided that they don't want children at all. Invalid reasons include the couple hoping that the operation will improve a shaky marriage or a sexual problem such as frigidity, impotence or premature ejaculation. There is some evidence that if the couple have previously enjoyed a good sex life, and it has only deteriorated because of the fear of pregnancy, then the problem *is* often solved by sterilization. However it will not magically provide a good sex life when the root of the problem is something else.

The decision to be sterilized should never be taken when the marriage is under pressure, e.g. when a personal or family crisis has built up, or immediately after a difficult pregnancy. Decisions taken at times of crisis may not be permanent; once the crisis is over, the sterilization may be bitterly regretted. Couples are also advised not to be sterilized while the wife is still carrying their last planned pregnancy; instead it is preferable to wait until the baby has arrived safely. Most doctors prefer to wait for a month or so in any case between the couple deciding on sterilization and the operation itself, to act as a time when the couple can either consolidate their decision or change their minds.

One very important element of counselling is what the couple will feel if the marriage breaks up, e.g through death, divorce or separation. Most people (Christians in particular) don't like to think of the possibility of any of these events, probably because it seems disloyal to be thinking of marrying someone else, but the issues must be faced. Another important decision is what they would do, and how they would feel, if one or more of their present children were to die. Would they then want to increase their family? Yet another large area of debate is, which partner should be sterilized? Vasectomy is quick and easy, and often makes a man feel that at last he can take a positive part in contraception. On the other hand, a man's ability to father a child lasts way beyond his wife's ability to conceive, which stops at the menopause. Therefore he may be more likely to expect to have children in the course of any second marriage.

The couple should also be reminded that even sterilization is not one hundred per cent effective as a means of contraception. Also, if the man or the woman has any doubts over the couple's future sex life, they should be reassured that sterilization will not affect sexuality if they are totally happy with the decision to be sterilized. All these issues should be discussed at length with one another and with the doctor, and should be prayed over before a couple makes the big decision to be sterilized. As Tim and Beverly La Haye say in *The Act of Marriage*: 'No Christian couple should ever take this operation lightly or rush into it without careful consideration.'

VASECTOMY

Vasectomy is, at the moment, the only reliable method of male sterilization. The operation has gained popularity since the 1950s, not least because it is simpler and safer than female sterilization (this was especially true when female sterilization was still a major operation).

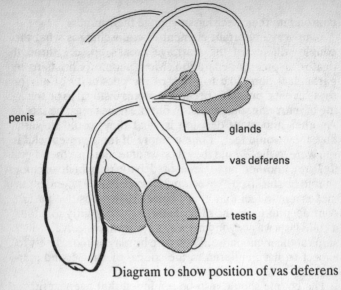

penis

glands

vas deferens

testis

Diagram to show position of vas deferens

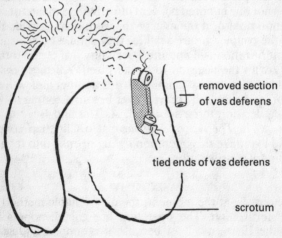

removed section of vas deferens

tied ends of vas deferens

scrotum

Diagram to show section of vas deferens being removed

Method

Vasectomy involves blocking or severing the two vas deferens, the tubes which transport the sperm inside the man's scrotum. The operation is a very straightforward surgical procedure, and is done under local anaesthetic. All the hairs on the scrotum and penis are cut very short, and the area is washed thoroughly. Two small incisions are made in the scrotum, one at each side. Through each incision the vas on that side is drawn and cut and tied; for extra surety the cut ends can be electrocoagulated. The vas is replaced and the incision is stitched with an absorbable suture. Recovery generally takes fifteen to thirty minutes, and then the patient can go home.

If you are planning a vasectomy, arrange for a friend or your wife to be available to drive you home; this helps to decrease complications. Plan to rest for forty-eight hours after the operation; if you put an ice pack on the scrotum for about four hours after the operation, this will reduce any swelling, bleeding or discomfort. Aspirin should be powerful enough to deal with any pain experienced. Avoid strenuous physical exercise for a week, and wear a scrotal support if it gives you extra comfort. Do not shower or bathe for forty-eight hours, and do not have sex for two to three days. After forty-eight hours, plain warm baths several times a day are ideal. The clinic should arrange for a check-up several weeks after the operation, and this should always be attended.

After a vasectomy you will still ejaculate normally, as sperm form only a small proportion of the seminal fluid. However, you will not immediately be sterile. Estimates vary as to just how long it takes to flush out any sperm that remain in the system; certainly a minimum of ten ejaculations, and some clinics say twenty. They will ask you to go back with a sample of ejaculate so that they can check whether the operation has been successful; again, clinics vary as to how many sperm-free samples they require before they feel that the man is fully sterile. Effectiveness after this point is over ninety-nine per cent.

Complications
At the moment there does not seem to be any major long-term complication of vasectomy other than very rare serious infections. The mortality rate is roughly 1 death in 100,000 operations, even under undesirable conditions (e.g. primitive clinics in developing countries). All complications together total only three per cent of patients, and are generally very minor such as swelling, discoloration and discomfort. Danger signs to be watched for after vasectomy are: fever (over 100.4°F), bleeding from the site of the incision, and excessive pain or swelling.

One controversial topic concerns sperm antibodies. Many men (between one and two-thirds of all vasectomy patients) form high levels of antibodies to their own sperm after the operation. These are formed as a reaction to the body's breakdown of sperm which are not released as normal because the vasectomy has blocked their path. In monkeys, high levels of sperm antibodies have been found to accelerate atherosclerosis, which can lead to disease of the circulatory system. However, five studies on humans have failed to find a similar connection. Some doctors do err on the side of caution and suggest that men with a high-risk history of cardiovascular disease should delay vasectomy until further studies are completed. Many other doctors feel that this is over-cautious.

There are a few other, though rare, contraindications for vasectomy. These include genital or scrotal infection, bleeding disorders, or being on anticoagulant therapy. Some conditions such as variocele, hydrocele, scrotal hernia, or present or past undescended testis may require treatment as a hospital inpatient, under general anaesthetic. Also some psychosexual conditions may be considered as contraindications.

Reversibility

Of course the ideal vasectomy operation is one that can be fully reversed when wished, but this is still a thing of the future, although much research is being done into the problem. Some practitioners prefer to clip the vas deferens rather than cutting it, in the hope that the clip can be successfully removed later, but this is not such an effective method of sterilization meanwhile. Actual success rates of reversal operations vary from eighteen to sixty per cent of selected patients – some patients may not even be suitable for selection for a possible reversal operation. Success is linked to the surgical procedure that was originally used, the length of the vas removed, the site of the incision, whether or not the cut ends of the vas were coagulated, what type of suture was used, and how long ago the operation was performed.

Even among those men whose ejaculate contains sperm after a reversal attempt their success in actually fathering a child is only fifty to seventy per cent: and this may take many months. Theoretically it should be possible to develop a clip, plug or valve which can be removed or reversed when desired, but the practical problems to be surmounted are vast. Therefore a vasectomy should always be considered as permanent if the operation is chosen; a man who goes into it in the belief that it can be reversed if he changes his mind is very likely to be disappointed.

Conclusions

Vasectomy is a very safe and simple method of contraception. It is extremely effective in preventing conception, and is an excellent option for a healthy husband who, with his wife, is quite sure that he never wishes to have any more children. The operation should not be considered reversible, and so the couple should receive detailed counselling and be very sure that this is the option they want before the operation is done. Vasectomy gives the husband a chance to take full responsibility for contraception, which can be a

131

boon when this has previously tended to be the lot of the wife. Vasectomy can be done under the NHS, or privately if you prefer or if there is a long NHS waiting list.

FEMALE STERILIZATION

The main principle of female sterilization involves cutting or blocking the fallopian tubes (see p. 19) so that the egg cannot be reached by the sperm. Over a hundred different ways of doing this have been developed; some are extremely successful, some less so, and some are associated with particular complications. The three main ways of occluding the tubes are: to cut them; to burn them with electrocoagulation; and to block them with clips, ties, bands, plugs or rings. Each of these methods has numerous variations; some of the most common are shown in the diagrams.

Methods
There are several ways of approaching the fallopian tubes to allow the sterilization to be carried out. Female sterilization used to require major abdominal surgery, but the development of new techniques and approaches means that this is no longer the case. The first method is by the mini-laparotomy, or mini-lap. This can be done under a local anaesthetic, or under spinal or general anaesthesia. A small (2-3cm) incision is made in the abdomen; through this the fallopian tube is grasped and occluded in the chosen way. The incision is stitched with absorbable sutures, then the patient rests for about two days. Strenuous activity should be avoided for a week or so.

The second approach is the laparoscopy. This generally is done under a general anaesthetic, but in some cases can be done under a local as an outpatient. A tiny incision (about 1cm) is made in the abdomen, then the abdominal cavity is inflated with gas to provide a larger, less cluttered working area. Special instruments are placed in the cavity through the incision; the surgeon can see the organs through the optical part of the instrument, and can manipulate the

132

other parts to occlude the tubes. An ordinary laparotomy (the old method of sterilization) requires a 10cm incision and a much longer hospital stay and recovery period. It also has a higher mortality rate. However this operation is sometimes necessary in place of a laparoscopy or mini-lap, if the woman is ill or has other abdominal complications.

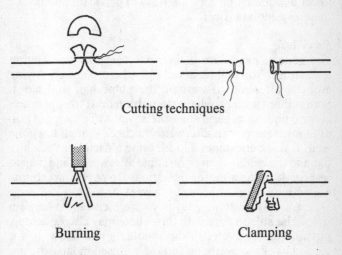

Cutting techniques

Burning   Clamping

Common techniques of sterilization

Two approaches have been developed for sterilizing via the vagina. Obviously this means that surgery through the abdominal wall is not required, and the operations have no visible scar. Culpotomy is an ordinary sterilization through the cul-de-sac of the vagina; culdoscopy uses the same approach, but is done with an endoscope (the same type of instrument used in a laparoscopy). A very rarely used method involves approaching the fallopian tubes via the cervix.

One method of sterilization which is not based on occluding the fallopian tubes is hysterectomy, the surgical removal of the uterus. This is a major operation, and is not usually justifiable simply for the purpose of sterilization. This is generally only performed where the uterus itself is diseased, for instance by cancer. Some conditions will be contraindications to abdominal sterilization; these can include cardiorespiratory problems, extreme obesity, previous lower abdominal surgery, a history of pelvic inflammation, or severe endometriosis.

Procedure

The general procedure is the same for most sterilization techniques. You will be asked to bathe or shower, paying especial attention to washing the pubic hair and navel. Some clinics prefer to shave the pubic hair. If the operation is done under a general anaesthetic you will be kept in hospital for a day or two afterwards to check that all has gone well. If it is done under a local, bring a friend or your husband to the clinic to drive you home afterwards, and plan to rest for 48 hours after the operation. Do not do any strenuous activity, sport or lifting for a week or so.

There may be some pain from the incision(s) – aspirin should be able to cope with this. There may also be aching, possibly quite severe, in the shoulders and chest; this is caused by the anaesthetic and the gas used in laparoscopy, but will disappear in 24-48 hours. Occasionally there will be pelvic aching or discomfort.

You will usually be told that you can bathe or shower at any time, but don't rub your stitches or incisions; pat dry carefully around that area. The clinic will ask you to return for a follow-up check about a month after the operation; it is important to attend. After a sterilization you will be completely protected from conception immediately, provided you did not ovulate in the 48 hours before surgery. If you did, the egg may already be in the lower part of the fallopian tube and available for fertilization, but most clinics will try to arrange the timing of your sterilization so that this is not a danger. You can resume sexual activity as soon as this feels comfortable; stop if you feel any discomfort or pain.

Complications

The mini-lap is generally a very safe operation with a very small percentage of complications (0.5-3% of all operations). Laparoscopy has a similar, or slightly higher, complication rate, although some of these can be related to the general anaesthetic rather than the specific operation. The mortality rate can be 1-10 per 100,000 (compared with up to 8 per 100,000 for mini-lap). Other complications of laparoscopy can include uterine perforation, bleeding, and bowel burns (from electrocoagulation). With both these approaches there is an almost total lack of infection, and they are much better than the vaginal approaches in this respect. Most of the complications can be prevented by careful attention to the surgical procedure.

Culpotomy has a complication rate twice as high as that for abdominal approaches. Ordinary laparotomy has a mortality rate of 10-25 per 100,000, and hysterectomy has a complication and mortality rate 10-100 times greater than that for mini-lap and laparoscopy.

After sterilization there is generally no change in the menstrual pattern. The ovaries are still functioning as normal, and the endometrium is building up and being shed in the same way. One possible, though very rare, complication of sterilization is failure of the operation – in other words, pregnancy! This can occur if the cut ends of the tube rejoin – this is more likely to occur with electrocoagulation than any of the other methods. The failure rate of sterilization is estimated at 0.25% over 4 years. If a woman does become pregnant as a result of sterilization failure, the pregnancy is very likely to be ectopic – some studies say the likelihood may be as high as 50%, compared with 0.5% of pregnancies among other women. Ectopic pregnancy can occur if the fallopian tube is partially blocked – the sperm may be able to get through to fertilize the egg, but the egg, being so much bigger than the sperm, may then not be able to continue down the tube. Ectopic pregnancy is, of course, a life-threatening condition.

Danger signs to be watched for after any sterilization are: fever (over 100.4°F); bleeding from the site of the incision; fainting spells; excessive pain or swelling; symptoms of pregnancy. If any of these occur, see a doctor immediately.

Reversibility
As with vasectomy, the ideal female sterilization operation is one that can be reversed without delay or problems when wished. Also as with vasectomy, this ideal is a long way off, although much research is working in this direction (see p. 146). The success of reversal tends to depend on how much of the fallopian tube is left; at least 3cm of one tube must exist to make the operation worthwhile. Electrocoagulation destroys the most tube, and is the hardest to reverse. Theoretically, plastic clips on the tubes should be the easiest method to reverse, but this is not as simple as it sounds. Tissue tends to grow over the clip, bonding it to the tube, and scar tissue can form in and on the tube itself, leaving it blocked or damaged even when the clip is removed.

Approximately 1% of all sterilization patients request a reversal. Of these, roughly 20% will be selected as suitable candidates; roughly 50% of those selected will have a successful reversal operation. Even when conception occurs, it may take many months, and there is three times the normal chance of failing to deliver a live baby. Once again, sterilization should always be considered permanent. The woman who has the operation in the hope that it can be reversed if she ever changes her mind is likely to be disappointed.

Conclusions
Female sterilization is generally a safe operation with a low rate of complications, although not quite as safe as vasectomy. It is a very effective means of preventing conception,

136

and once the operation has been done there is no need to take any further contraceptive precautions. It used to be the case that sterilization would only be performed if the woman's age multiplied by the number of children she had was 120 or more (for example if she was twenty-five with five children, or thirty with four). This is no longer the case, and if you are a healthy woman who has decided, with your husband, that you do not intend to bear any more children, sterilization may well be a valid option for you. Sterilization is available on the NHS, but it can be done privately if you prefer or if the NHS waiting list is too long.

12

Faith alone

Some Christian couples choose to rely entirely on prayer to limit the size of their family. This can take two forms. One way is not to use any kind of contraception and simply to trust God that whatever children he gives are his will for that couple. The other way is to decide prayerfully how many children you want, and then to trust God to give you that number in his timing. The issue seems to me to be a little akin to healing. There is no doubt that God can heal miraculously in answer to prayer. There is also no doubt that at times he doesn't. At times he directs us to use the medical wisdom of doctors and specialists who are able to achieve healing through drugs or surgery. And sometimes there is no healing.

God has given us many methods of contraception, of which contraception through prayer alone is only one. For some couples it has undoubtedly worked; that does not necessarily mean that it is the right method for you. Contraception through prayer is not any more or less worthy, or more or less 'Christian' than contraception by conventional methods. It is important that couples who feel they want to use this method are specifically called to it by God – otherwise they are almost certain to find themselves with a baby disturbingly early in their marriage, or with more children than they can afford or handle. In these cases, their faith may take a tumble from which it will be difficult to recover, and they may blame God for their own carelessness.

Joyce Huggett, in *Growing into Love*, says that shifting the responsibility for contraception onto God's shoulders is 'rather like walking into the middle of the road in front of oncoming traffic, trusting God for protection. God delights to protect his children. He also expects adults to behave as adults, to use their common sense and to exercise the freedom of choice with which he invested them.' Believing that God *can* limit families by prayer is not enough. If you use this method, you need to be totally convinced that God is specifically calling you to limit *your* family by prayer. You cannot just casually throw caution to the wind and expect God to take on a responsibility that he may be expecting you to take on.

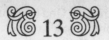

13

New Developments

The search still continues for the perfect contraceptive. Some of the research is directed at developing totally new concepts in birth control, but any entirely new method would have to pass such stringent evaluations that it would be unlikely to be available widely before the end of the century. Much more of the research is being directed at improving the reliability and acceptability of existing methods. This chapter is a summary of major birth control developments and possibilities at the time of writing. Some of these methods will never succeed, or will never obtain full medical or social acceptance. Others may be made available within the next few years. Some methods will open up new ethical dilemmas for Christians – others will be welcomed wholeheartedly.

BARRIER METHODS

Contracap. This is a barrier method designed by a gynaecologist and a dentist. A custom-made rubber cap is produced from a mould of the woman's cervix, and is such a close fit that it remains in place on the cervix through surface tension alone. The cap contains a one-way valve which, theoretically, allows the menstrual flow out but prevents sperm from reaching the uterus. Researchers hope that the cap could be left in place for months at a time.

NSFFD. These initials stand for 'no spermicide, fit-free diaphragm' method. An American doctor is researching the possibility of using a single size of diaphragm for all women, without spermicide. The diaphragm is worn continuously, and removed once a day for washing.

Starch polymers. One suggested way of blocking the vagina is with a gel-forming polymer which expands as it absorbs moisture from the vagina. Spermicides could be incorporated for extra safety.

Spermicides. Most spermicides contain nonoxynol-9 as the main sperm-killing agent. Other substances are being researched which inhibit the enzymes that enable the sperm to penetrate, and so fertilize, the ovum.

IVD. Intra-vaginal devices are cylinders of silicone rubber rather like menstrual tampons. They are impregnated with spermicide, and designed to be worn for about a month.

Hydrophilic sheaths. These are sheaths made from a substance which absorbs moisture; the intention is that the sheath then feels more like natural skin to the man and the woman.

RHYTHM METHODS

Ovulation predictors. The main problem in the rhythm methods is in predicting when ovulation is going to take place, and to give sufficient warning to avoid sex in the 'unsafe' days before that time. Ways being tested of accurately predicting ovulation include miniature computers checking the basal body temperature, and urine testers. The urine testing kits act on the 'dipstick' principle to test for the metabolites of certain hormones; as these levels rise, the dipsticks show the warning colours.

Ovutime Tackiness Rheometer. This is a mechanical device which measures the consistency of the cervical mucus.

Ultrasound. Ultrasound scans can be used to detect and monitor the growth and rupture of the follicle, although this method could not easily be made generally available.

Tail-less IUDs.   These are very popular in the East. Tail-less IUDs are now being tested in the Western world as it is thought that they might reduce the incidence of infection. One theory is that infective agents travel up the IUD tail-strings and so into the uterus.

Post-partum IUDs   Fitting IUDs in women who have just given birth tends to be difficult as the expulsion rate is high. It is possible that this could be overcome by using biode-gradable sutures or prongs to anchor the IUD to the uterus wall until the uterus has regained its customary shape and size.

Anderson leaf.   This is a silicone rubber IUD impregnated with copper or zinc or both.

Levonorgestrel-releasing IUD.   This is the one IUD which seems, on all the evidence available so far, to work by pre-venting the passage of the sperm into the uterus. The IUD is coated in silastic material impregnated with the drug, which is then released slowly. It seems to act as a cervical barrier to bacteria as well as to sperm, and this IUD also seems to reduce menstrual bleeding and spotting. This IUD could be very good news for women who would like the efficiency of an IUD but who also want to prevent concep-tion rather than implantation.

ICDs.   Intra-cervical devices, as their name suggests, are worn in the cervical canal; small arms protrude into the uterus to help hold the device in place. The ICD is covered in a drug reservoir – chemicals being tested include sper-micides, norgestrol and norethindrone. It seems from ani-mal tests that the presence of higher levels of progestogens actually in the cervical mucus prevent sperm migration and so prevent fertilization, even though ovulation has taken place. Lower levels appear to work by preventing implan-tation of the fertilized ovum.

Vaginal rings. Quite extensive tests have been carried out on rings worn around the cervix at the top of the vagina. The rings are worn for 21 days at a time, then removed for 7 days for a breakthrough bleeding. Each ring contains enough chemical to last for at least six months. Different chemicals have been tried. Some (norethindrone and norgestrol) can inhibit ovulation; others use progestogens to alter the cervical mucus and/or inhibit the sperm. Other trials have used spermicide. Effectiveness in trials with progestogens is around 98%. Some trials have used rings containing oestrogens as well as progestogens – interestingly natural progestogens can be absorbed via this route although they cannot be taken orally, which may reduce the potential oestrogen-related problems. Some organizations are researching a ring which could be left in place for three months.

Postage-stamp pill. Some women have difficulty in swallowing tablets, however small, so some researchers are working on impregnating the chemicals into a substance like rice-paper. The woman simply tears off and eats a square each day!

Monthly pills. These are not, unfortunately, contraceptive pills which need to be taken only once a month. Rather they are a postcoital method; the researchers are trying to find a drug regime which can be used to produce bleeding once a month, even if conception has taken place, thus inducing an early abortion. The drugs may work by interfering with the corpus luteum, or by causing uterine contractions to expel the pregnancy.

Postcoital pessaries. These use prostaglandins in a vaginal pessary to induce an early abortion.

Monthly injectables. These take various forms in trials done so far. The main types are progestogen-only, and oestrogen and progestogen. The progestogen-only regimes are similar to the other injectables (see p. 79) but at shorter intervals. The addition of oestrogen reduces menstrual disruption and appears to produce one hundred per cent effectiveness – presumably the addition of oestrogen also helps to prevent ovulation. Oestrogen cannot be used in injection regimes longer than a month, as its effect diminishes rapidly; also it is not advisable to expose the body to three months' dosage of oestrogen in one go. Data on monthly injectables are scant, but one formulation (known as injectable No 1) accounts for one per cent of all contraceptive use in the Peoples' Republic of China.

Implants.   One of the big objections to implanted contraceptives is that the capsules have to be removed when the drug is used up. Biodegradable capsules are being researched which will disintegrate harmlessly at the end of the drug regime.

Biodegradables.   Biodegradables are being researched to meet the demand for carriers of long-acting hormones (or other substances) which will release at a constant rate into the body, and also be broken down by the body when the drug is used up. In some cases, if the delivery system is near the reproductive organs, much lower doses than usual can be used (1/10th or even 1/100th) as the drug does not have to pass through the liver, which metabolizes a large proportion. Many of the combined pill's adverse effects are thought to be the result of having to use such high doses – local injections of biodegradables could side-step this problem.

Some of the delivery systems tried are:

Microcapsules – small synthetic hollow cells containing the drug.
Microsponges – microscopic membranes with lots of pockets to hold the drug.
Microspheres – solid beads of polymer with the drug dispersed in the material or used to coat the surface.

Erythrocyte ghosts – red blood cells which have been emptied then refilled with the drug and resealed.
Liposomes – tiny particles which coat a liquid-based drug.

The carriers may be taken by mouth, via vaginal pessaries, or injected into the bloodstream, under the skin, into the muscles, or into the peritoneal cavity. All of these systems are still in the early stages of research.

Nasal spray. This method of contraception is based on daily sniffs of LHRH (luteinising hormone releasing hormone). The hormone has been tested on both males and females. In women it can prevent ovulation, and also make the body unable to sustain a pregnancy. It does also seem to interrupt the menstrual cycle in some women.

Male hormonal contraception. Putting out of action the millions of sperm produced every day by the average man is not easy, which is one reason why male hormonal contraception lags far behind similar developments for women. Also, sperm formation and storage takes about three months, so effects would not be noticeable until after that time.

Gossypol has become notorious as a potential male pill; it was isolated and extracted from cottonseed after extensive research linked an outbreak of male infertility in China with the consumption of food cooked in cottonseed oil. Since 1972 over 4,000 men have been treated with gossypol tablets; a very low sperm count, low enough to prevent conception, occurred in up to ninety-nine per cent of the men treated. The drug suppresses sperm production and also alters the structure and motility of any sperm that are formed. Potential side-effects include decreased libido, nausea, changes in appetite, weakness, and lowered blood potassium levels. In high doses the drug can induce cardiac irregularities. Fertility appears to return completely after a few months without the drug.

LHRH (luteinising hormone releasing hormone) has

also been tried as a male contraceptive. Both of these drugs will require many more years of satisfactory tests before they could be approved for general use. A further method being investigated involves administration of a drug which immobilizes the sperm or causes them to agglutinate – clump together.

Vaccination. The concept of vaccination against pregnancy is based on producing antibodies that either block conception or prevent implantation. Some antibodies work on the zona pellucida around the ovum and prevent fertilization from occurring – these have been used to produce short-term and long-term infertility in animals. Other antibodies work to destroy the corpus luteum, and so prevent successful implantation of the fertilized egg.

Abortion pill. A pill has been developed in France that induces abortion in early pregnancy.

FEMALE STERILIZATION
Many methods have been found to block the fallopian tubes, and many more are being researched. The introduction of various chemicals into the uterus via the vagina and cervix can block the tubes without the need for an operation. Chemicals tested include silver nitrate, zinc chloride, phenol, plastic and silicate blocking agents, and tissue adhesives. Also an IUD which releases a blocking agent is being tested. Other trials have blocked the tubes using heat cauterization or cryosurgery (freezing) via the vagina and uterus rather than the abdomen. Another method uses a uterine reservoir containing a viscous liquid; every time the uterus contracts, the liquid is slowly pushed up the tubes.

Reversibility is always an ideal of sterilization operations, and various devices are being tested with this in mind including one rather like a rawplug and screw! Others consist of silicone plugs that cure in situ, but have a retrieval loop on the uterine end. Still other techniques use plastic or silastic meshes in the fallopian tubes.

146

14

Conclusions

So, after all this information, what can we deduce about the role of contraception in a Christian marriage?

First of all, we have seen that sex within marriage is a part of God's good plan for humankind, and that it is not right just to restrict it to procreation. Every couple has the justification, if they choose, to enjoy this part of their marriage without a constant fear of pregnancy. Contraception is one of the factors which makes this full enjoyment possible. There is no biblical argument which prohibits the use of contraception.

The thoughtful use of contraception also helps to protect the health of the woman between children, and the health of subsequent children. It also helps the couple to avoid the emotional, financial and even spiritual strains of conceiving a child too soon or at the wrong time. From the point of view of Christians as world citizens, it also helps to keep a small check on the national and worldwide population level.

However, there is no perfect contraceptive. The perfect method would be one hundred per cent effective, totally and instantly reversible, ethically unquestionable, would not interrupt lovemaking, and would have no side-effects or extra effects whatsoever on wife, husband or subsequent children. As Guillebaud says: 'All our present reversible methods are tried and found wanting in some way.' All have drawbacks – some are not reversible, some are messy, some are unethical, some can be dangerous, some interfere with sex, some are unreliable, some delay the return of fertility, and so on and so on. Research is constantly trying to minimize these drawbacks, but like most things in this world, contraception is always going to present problems.

Nevertheless the acceptable choices are still numerous for most couples, and you may not want to use the same method for every stage of your marriage. Some methods will suit your own preferences, age, stage of marriage and lifestyles more than others. You have to weigh up the risks and benefits of each method and make your choice before God. Tim and Beverly La Haye say: 'Realistically speaking, each couple should prayerfully and thoughtfully bring into the world the number of children they can properly train to serve God.' I hope that the main sections of this book have made this aim easier and helped to point the way through the maze of family planning material available today. The questionnaire which follows may help you to choose exactly which options you feel happy with.

What if you have been using, or have used in the past, a method of birth control that you now see may have grieved God, or been wrong in his sight? It is very important not to blame yourself for things you didn't know. If you were acting in good faith, and responsibly, on the information you had, God will honour you for that, and you must not be overcome by guilt feelings. By all means ask God for his forgiveness if you feel that you have wronged him in this way, and accept his forgiveness freely with open arms, just as he accepts you. Then re-examine your options in the light of the new information you have access to, and make your choice together – husband, wife and God.

Questionnaire

This section is designed to help point you towards the contraceptive alternatives that might be best for you as a couple at this stage of your marriage. It is not intended to make the choice for you; this must be done together and with God. Rather it is a summary of the information contained in the main sections of the book, and will help you to clarify your own thoughts and work out whether a particular contraceptive suits you emotionally, physically, psychologically and spiritually. If you answer yes to any question, the comments underneath will be relevant to your choice of contraceptive.

Questions for husband and wife

Are you relaxed with each other sexually?
You will probably be happy to cope with a cap, sheath, spermicide or sponge. If you are not relaxed in this way, avoid methods that need to be used at the time of sex.

Is it very important to you not to get pregnant just now?
You will need to use a very reliable contraceptive such as the pill, or a less reliable method (such as a cap or sheath) very conscientiously. Do not use a spermicide alone, sponges, breastfeeding, withdrawal or rhythm methods.

Is it very important to you never to become pregnant again?
Sterilization is the most effective option in this case, either female sterilization or vasectomy.

Are you newly married?
You may find it preferable to use a safe, unembarrassing method

such as the combined pill while you get to know one another.

Are you happy with hormonal contraceptives?
Possibilities include the combined pill, the mini-pill, injectables and implants. If you are not keen on hormonal methods, caps, sheaths, sponges, spermicides and rhythm methods will suit you better.

Are you just trying to delay pregnancy rather than prevent it altogether?
You may be happy with a less reliable method such as barrier methods, rhythm methods or even breastfeeding.

Would you like a long-term contraceptive?
The longest-acting reversible methods are injectables, implants and IUDs.

Do you want to avoid methods that interfere with implantation rather than preventing conception?
Do not use an IUD, and think carefully before using the mini-pill, implants or injectables.

Do you prefer not to limit sex to infertile times?
Avoid the rhythm methods.

Would you like a method that requires no medical intervention?
The possible choices are spermicides, sheaths, rhythm methods, withdrawal, breastfeeding and sponges.

Is either of you allergic to rubber?
You will need to avoid some brands of sheath and cap.

Is either of you allergic to spermicide?
Barrier methods will not be suitable, unless you can find a brand of spermicide to which you are not sensitive.

Questions for husband

Are you willing to take the main responsibility for contraception?
Sheaths and vasectomy are the major forms of male contraceptive.

150

Do you suffer from premature ejaculation?
The sheath may help overcome this problem, as it reduces sensitivity. If you do suffer from premature ejaculation, don't use the withdrawal method or spermicide alone.

Do you have any of the following conditions: cardiovascular disease, bleeding disorders, scrotal infection?
It is probably advisable to avoid vasectomy.

Are you considerably older than your wife, or in poor health?
If you as a couple are considering sterilization, vasectomy might be preferable to female sterilization.

Do you suffer from any of the following: undescended testis (or history of), variocele, hydrocele, scrotal hernia?
These conditions may complicate any vasectomy operation.

Questions for wife

Are you in your thirties or forties?
The pill is less safe for you than for younger women. As your fertility is lower, barrier methods are more reliable than for younger women. If you have completed your family, sterilization might be a good option.

Are you happy to take the main responsibility for contraception?
If so, the options are the combined pill, the mini-pill, implants, injectables, IUDs, rhythm methods, caps, sponges, spermicides and female sterilization.

Do you have any condition which does, or could, require frequent surgery or bed-rest?
Avoid the combined pill.

Are you scared of pregnancy?
You will need a very reliable contraceptive method, such as the combined pill, to set your mind at rest.

Are you overweight or a heavy smoker?
You should probably avoid the pill.

Do you have little natural lubrication during sex?
A method which involves using spermicide (any of the barrier methods) can provide extra lubrication.

Do you suffer from a prolapse, unusually-positioned uterus, rectocele, cystocele, or poor muscle tone in the vagina?
You will probably not be suited to a diaphragm or sponge.

Do you have any erosion or abnormality of the cervix?
You will not be able to use a cervical cap.

Do you suffer from cystitis?
This may possibly be aggravated by the diaphragm or by the combined pill.

Do you feel uncomfortable about touching your genitals?
You will not find caps, sponges or spermicides easy to use.

Do you suffer from bad pre-menstrual tension?
The combined pill would virtually eradicate this condition.

Are you forgetful?
If so, it is best not to use a contraceptive pill at all, and definitely not the mini-pill or phased pills. If you are determined to use a pill, the 28-day pill is best.

Do you suffer from epilepsy or TB?
Some of the drugs used to treat these conditions may interfere with the combined pill.

Do you regularly take large doses of vitamin C?
Avoid the combined pill.

Do you take any medication for diabetes, anxiety, depression, high blood pressure or migraine?
Some (but not all) of these may be affected by the contraceptive pill.

Are you breastfeeding?
Avoid the combined pill, as this suppresses lactation. The mini-pill, IUD, injectables, rhythm methods and barrier methods do not affect lactation.

Do you wear contact lenses?
This might be affected by using the combined pill, as the fluid over the cornea is altered.

Have you ever suffered from ovarian cysts, endometriosis, or non-malignant breast disease?
The combined pill may help protect against further incidents of these conditions.

Do you have, or have you ever had, breast cancer?
Only use hormonal contraceptives if your specialist approves.

Do you have an irregular menstrual cycle?
If so, the rhythm methods are not recommended. If your irregular periods are a problem, they can be regulated by using the combined pill, but this may be preferable only after you have completed your family.

Do you have, or have a history of, any of these conditions: thrombosis, stroke, coronary artery disease, breast cancer, hepatic disease, cancer of the reproductive system?
You must not use the combined pill, or (probably) the mini-pill.

Do you suffer from any of the following: very severe migraine, sickle-cell anaemia, angina, pituitary gland disorder, recent molar pregnancy, undiagnosed uterine bleeding?
You must not use the combined pill, or (probably) the mini-pill.

Do you have any of the following conditions: diabetes, family history of cardiovascular disease, severe fluid retention, severe headaches, scanty periods, gallbladder disease, Gilbert's disease, severe asthma or epilepsy, severe varicose veins, high blood pressure?
The combined pill may not be a good choice for you. For those with headaches and high blood pressure, the mini-pill is safer than the combined pill.

Are you underweight?
If so, you are more likely to experience nausea if using the combined pill, and stand a higher chance of becoming pregnant accidentally if you use NET-EN injectable.

Do you suffer from any abnormal uterine bleeding, or have a history of ectopic pregnancy?
Do not use the mini-pill or IUD.

Have you ever had pelvic inflammatory disease?
Do not use an IUD. The combined pill may help protect against a further attack.

Do you suffer from anaemia, heavy periods, large numbers of fibroids, small or abnormal uterus, severe cervicitis, painful periods?
Do not use an IUD. Heavy and painful periods can be eased greatly by the combined pill, but this pill may accelerate the degeneration of fibroids.

Do you suffer from cardiorespiratory problems, extreme obesity, a history of lower abdominal surgery, pelvic inflammation, or severe endometriosis?
Female sterilization is not recommended.

Glossary

Abortifacient – a substance or procedure which induces an abortion.

Abortion – death of a foetus before 28 weeks of the pregnancy. This can be either spontaneous or artificially induced.

Anaemia – a deficiency of iron in the blood.

Barrier methods – methods of contraception which put a physical barrier between sperm and ova.

Blastocyst – fertilized ovum.

Capacitation – the process which enables sperm to fertilize an ovum; this takes place as sperm swim through the female reproductive tract.

Castration – surgical removal of the testes.

Cervical erosion – a sore or rough place on the cervix.

Cervix – the neck of the uterus.

Coil – another name for the IUD.

Coitus interruptus – the withdrawal method of contraception.

Combined pills – oral contraceptives containing oestrogen and progestogen.

Conception – the fertilization of an ovum by a sperm.

Condom – another common name for the sheath.

Contraindication – a characteristic or a medical condition which means that you are, or may be, unsuited to a particular method of birth control.

Corpus luteum – the name given to the empty egg follicle after ovulation.

Culdoscopy – an endoscopic procedure which can be used for sterilization via the vagina.

Culpotomy – a procedure which can be used for sterilization via the vagina.

Cystitis – infection of the bladder.

D&C – dilatation and curettage, sometimes used as a method of abortion.

D&E – dilatation and evacuation, a method of abortion.

Depo-Provera – the most common form of the injectable contraceptive DMPA.

DMPA – an injectable progestogen contraceptive.

Dysmenorrhoea – painful periods.

Ectopic pregnancy – a pregnancy where the fertilized egg implants in the fallopian tube instead of in the uterus.

Ejaculation – the male orgasm, when the seminal fluid is released from the penis.

Electrocoagulation – a method of sterilization involving using heat on the fallopian tubes.

Endometriosis – a condition in which the endometrium cells grow outside the uterus in the pelvic cavity.

Endometritis –inflammation of the lining of the uterus.

Endometrium – the lining of the uterus.

Fallopian tubes – the tubes which carry the ova from the ovaries to the uterus.

Fertilization – the moment when a sperm fuses with an egg.

Follicle – the part of the ovary containing an egg.

FSH – follicle stimulating hormone, a female hormone.

HCG – human chorionic gonadotrophin, a hormone released during pregnancy.

Hydatidiform mole – a rare, but serious, 'fake' pregnancy, which can become malignant.

Hysterectomy – surgical removal of the uterus.

Hysterotomy – an operation through the wall of the uterus, which can be used as an abortion technique.

Implantation – the attachment of the fertilized ovum to the wall of the uterus.

IPPF – International Planned Parenthood Federation.

IUD – intra-uterine device, a method of birth control.

Labia – the folds of skin around the female genitals.

Lactation – the production of milk in a woman's breasts.

Laparoscopy – an endoscopic method of female sterilization.

Laparotomy – a small incision in the abdomen through which female sterilization can be performed.

Libido – sex drive.

Ligation – the blocking, tying, burning or cutting of the fallopian tubes in female sterilization.

LH – luteinising hormone, a female reproductive hormone.

Mini-lap – a very small abdominal incision through which female sterilization can be performed.

Mittelschmerz – the 'mid-pain' experienced by some women at ovulation.

Molar pregnancy – hydatidiform mole.

NET-EN – an injectable progestogen contraceptive.

NORPLANT – an implanted hormonal contraceptive.

Oestrogen – a female hormone, also contained in combined pills.

Oral contraceptives – hormonal contraceptives taken by mouth – mainly the combined pill and mini-pill.

Os – the mouth of the cervix.

Ovulation – the monthly release of a ripe ovum.

Ovum/ova – egg/eggs produced by the woman.

Pap smear – a cervical smear taken to check for pre-cancerous cells.

PID – pelvic inflammatory disease.

Pituitary – a gland at the base of the brain, responsible for controlling the sex hormones in men and women.

Post-coital methods – methods of birth control employed after conception, or after unprotected sex when conception may have taken place.

Progesterone – a female hormone.

Progestogen or progestin – synthetic progesterone.

Rhythm methods – methods of birth control which involve abstaining from sex during the woman's fertile days.

Speculum – an instrument for viewing the vagina and cervix.

Sperm – the male reproductive agents, released in the seminal fluid.

Spermicide – a chemical which kills or immobilizes sperm.

Spinnbarkeit – the 'stretchability' of the cervical mucus around the time of ovulation.

Sterilization – an operation intended to make a man or woman incapable of having children.

Uterine sound – an instrument used to measure the size of the uterus.

Uterus – womb.

Vacuum curettage – a method of abortion.

Vagina – the passage from the uterus to the external female genitals.

Vaginitis – infection of the vagina.

Vas deferens – the tube in the male testis which carries sperm.

Vasectomy – male sterilization, involving cutting or blocking the vas.

VD – venereal disease, or sexually transmitted disease.

WHO – World Health Organization.

Bibliography

Banks, B., and Banks, S., *Ministering to Abortion's Aftermath*. Impact Books Inc. 1982.

Barcelona *et al.*, *Contraception*. University of Chicago 1981.

Cauthery, P., Stanway, P., and Stanway, A., *The Complete Book of Love and Sex*. Century Publishing 1983.

Cowper, A., and Young, C., *Family Planning: Fundamentals for Health Professionals*. Croom Helm 1981.

Edelman *et al.*, *Intrauterine Devices and Their Complications*. Martinus Nijhoff 1979.

Gardner, R.F.R., *Moral Dilemmas in Contraceptive Developments*. Christian Medical Fellowship 1973.

Hafez, E.S., and Audebert, A.J., eds., *IUD Technology*. MTP Press 1982.

Hall, R., *Marie Stopes*. Andre Deutsch 1977.

Hall, R., *Dear Dr Stopes*. Andre Deutsch 1978.

Hatcher *et al.*, *Contraceptive Technology*. Irvington 1982.

Huggett, J., *Growing into Love*. IVP 1982.

Kane, P., *The Which? Guide to Birth Control*. Consumers' Association/Hodder and Stoughton 1983.

Keith *et al.*, *The Safety of Fertility Control*. Springer 1980.

Lader, L., and Meltzer, M., *Margaret Sanger*. Crowell 1969.

La Haye, T., and La Haye, B., *The Act of Marriage*. Zondervan 1980.

Marston, P., *God and the Family*. Kingsway 1984.

Melinsky, H., *Foreword to Marriage*. CIO Publishing 1984.

Miles, H.J., *Sexual Happiness in Marriage*. Zondervan 1982.

Morgan, M., *The Total Woman*. Hodder and Stoughton 1981.

Morris, N., and Arthure, H., *Sterilization as a Means of Birth Control in Men and Women*. Peter Owen 1976.

Noble, J., *Hide and Sex*. Kingsway 1981.

Nofziger, M., *A Cooperative Method of Natural Birth Control*. The Book Publishing Company 1978.

Patey, E., *I Give You This Ring*. Mowbray 1982.

Porter *et al.*, *The Health Provider's Guide to Contraception*. The Pathfinder Fund 1983.

Saidi, M.H., and Zainie, C.M., *Female Sterilization: A Handbook for Women*. Garland STPM Press 1980.

Shapiro, H.I., *The Birth Control Book*. Penguin Books 1980.

Smith, M., *Woman's Own Birth Control*. Hamlyn 1980.

Snowdon *et al.*, *The IUD - a Practical Guide*. Croom Helm 1977.

Townsend, A.J., *Families Without Pretending*. Scripture Union 1981.

Trobisch, I., *The Joy of Being a Woman*. Editions Trobisch 1977.

Wenham, and Winter, *Abortion: The Biblical and Medical Challenges*. Care Trust 1983.

Wheeler, R.J., ed., *Intrauterine Devices*. Academic Press 1974.

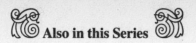

Creativity
Using your talents
EILEEN MITSON AND OTHERS

'In the beginning God created …'
and we, his children, made in his image,
also have the desire to create.
Creativity is God's gift to us.

If therefore our lives are open to him,
he will show us areas in every aspect of life
in which we can create new growth –
our homes, families and environment,
in our relationships and in our own
personalities and talents.
He has already provided us with the raw materials –
we can use them to build or destroy –
we can choose to be on the side of life, or of death.

Nine women who have chosen life
have contributed to this thought provoking book,
which will inspire every Christian woman
to explore new ideas and to develop
her own unique creative potential.

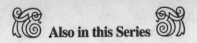

A Woman's Privilege

JEAN BRAND

The modern Christian woman
is often confused about her place in the world.
Secular pressures have blurred the
divisions between male and female roles.
Is this in line with God's plan for women?
Or does he require a woman to submerge
her whole personality
in submission to her husband?
And what about single women?

Jean Brand affirms that the Bible
represents a far more glorious pattern
and shows in a practical way, how every woman
can use her individuality and experience
to become the person God intends her to be.

Christian Woman

The Positive Alternative!

Do you want a magazine that is packed with stimulating, thought-provoking, amusing, helpful, informative and challenging articles?

Do you want a magazine that has the strength to stand out against a godless world?

Do you want a positive alternative to ordinary women's magazines?

Then you need *Christian Woman*!

Christian Woman monthly features interviews, debates, cookery, regular columnists, health and fashion, letters, news, crafts, overseas reports, book choice, reviews, music, spiritual focus page, fiction, leisure, poetry, and testimonies of God's power to change people's lives.

It will help you and encourage you to face the challenges of living as a Christian woman in today's world.

For a postal subscription for a year, send a cheque for £11 with your name and address to Christian Woman Sales Centre, 27 Chapel Road, Worthing, West Sussex BN11 1EG.